Jenny Oxton

The Student's Cookbook

Jenny Baker's interest in food began in her Devonshire grandmother's kitchen. During the sixties she lived with her husband James – who claims to have taught her how to cook – in the Middle East, and on their return to London they started a business catering for functions of up to 400 guests. When their son and daughter left home for college Jenny began to write about cooking. She divides her time between her two kitchens in London and France, and is now working on her new book *Kettle Broth to Gooseberry Fool*, also to be published by Faber.

The Student's Cookbook

Jenny Baker

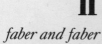

faber and faber

For Mark and Madeleine

First published in 1985
by Faber and Faber Limited
3 Queen Square London WC1N 3AU
This new edition published in 1996

Printed in England by Clays Ltd, St Ives plc

© Jenny Baker, 1985, 1996

Jenny Baker is hereby identified as author of this
work in accordance with Section 77 of the Copyright,
Designs and Patents Act 1988

A CIP record for this book
is available from the British Library

ISBN 0-571-17646-1

10 9 8 7 6 5 4 3 2 1

Contents

Introduction

The original version of this book was written over twelve years ago when my son and daughter went to college, which meant living away from home and fending for themselves. Both had hearty appetites but not much knowledge of cooking and, as at that time there were no cookery books written specifically with students in mind, I began to jot down recipes and collect ideas, bearing in mind that money was tight and that basically what they needed were things to cook which would not cost the earth and, just as important, wouldn't take hours to prepare. The result was *The Student's Cookbook*.

Things haven't got any easier. Students still have to feed themselves on a tight budget, tighter than it was when the book first came out. The grant cheque has to stretch further than ever and good eating can take second place to all those other expenses like rents, fares and books. Relying on take-aways, fizzy drinks and chocolate bars is bad for you and has become prohibitively expensive, so it's more essential than ever to know how to spend your food budget and how best to cook what you buy.

The positive news remains the same. You don't have to use expensive foods to live well. In fact some of the pricier things are not necessarily all that good for you. A diet consisting of plenty of fruit and vegetables, fish, white meat like chicken, pulses and some dairy products, augmented with pastas, rice and other grains, bread and potatoes need not be too costly. And don't worry about those carbohydrates being fattening: they're not, unless you eat them with lashings of the real fatteners like butter or margarine or sweet things like jams and marmalades.

A student's kitchen is hardly ever ideal. You have to learn to be adaptable and not get too resentful when for the umpteenth time you're faced with someone else's washing up or you go to the fridge only to discover that the phantom milk drinker has been at it again. So I've taken into account you may have to clear a corner of the work surface just to prepare your food and that conditions are likely to be the opposite of perfect, which means most of the recipes use a limited amount of space and cooking utensils. However, some in the section on *Group cooking* do stretch this point. They're fun to do if you find yourself sharing with people who also like to cook and are willing to take turns with the meals.

In this revised edition, I have updated many of the recipes and included some of the ingredients that weren't available when the book was first written. My original aim was to include as many different ideas as I possibly could in order to trigger off your own culinary inventions. I haven't abandoned this intention but I've approached the problem in a different way and given far more detailed instructions than before.

This isn't a cookery textbook and I've tried to keep these instructions very straightforward for those who've hardly ever done any cooking. If you're not in this category, bear with me as you may find some things are painfully obvious. Perhaps this is the moment to observe that preparing food is a creative process and there are as many ways of cooking as there are cooks. I hope this book will give you lots of ideas and satisfying meals, inspire you to experiment and by so doing will open up a whole new aspect of life.

So, here's to good cooking and good eating too!

Jenny Baker 1996

Culinary know-how

Good food
Equipment
Shopping choice
Buying and storing
Quantities, measurements and temperatures

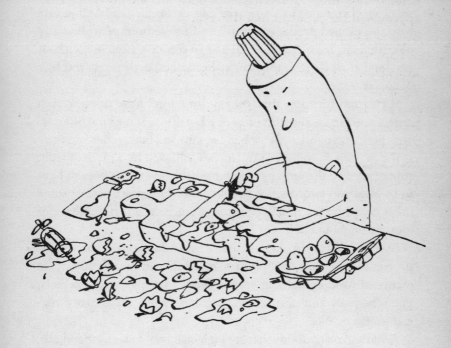

Good food

As a student living on very little money, your main concern will be how to get enough food for as little outlay as possible. Whether it is good in either the moral or the health sense may seem of secondary importance. However, it is encouraging to know that it is possible to eat well without having to spend an absolute fortune. It does mean of course being prepared to do some cooking and not relying on a daily diet of convenience foods, take-aways and pre-packaged meals.

Ideally, we should eat three meals a day to keep us ticking over comfortably. However, it doesn't matter if you prefer to eat lots of small snacks as long as these aren't an exclusive diet of chocolate bars and canned drinks which fill you up without providing any nourishment. It's not a good idea to go for long stretches without any food at all. This simply causes headaches, drowsiness and lack of concentration.

If you aim for three meals a day, you don't have to cook each time. Breakfast can be fruit juice or a hot drink, some kind of cereal with perhaps yogurt and some added nuts and fruit; lunch might be at the canteen or could be sandwiches followed by a piece of fruit; supper need be the only meal you have to cook and it doesn't have to be meat and two veg but could be based on pasta, rice or some other cereal with a quickly prepared sauce. You'll find plenty of ideas throughout the book.

Base your diet on making sure that every day you eat some high-protein food such as fish, poultry, meat, cheese, eggs or pulses; eat plenty of food containing carbohydrates such as bread, cereals, potatoes, pasta and rice; eat as much fresh fruit and as many vegetables as you like.

Avoid too many foods that are high in animal fats, sugar and salt. Although we do need some fat, we can cut down on our intake by using low-fat dairy produce and buying fats and oils which are labelled polyunsaturated. Sugar does provide instant energy but no nutrients. Better by far to eat plenty of other kinds of carbohydrate foods like bread, potatoes, pasta and cereals, which will make you feel satisfyingly full as well as increasing your energy. They won't make you gain weight, it's the lashings of butter, fats and sugary spreads that have this effect. As well as these carbohydrate foods, also eat plenty of nuts, fruits and pulses, all of which help the digestive system work well and keep teeth and gums healthy too, as they encourage chewing!

The table that follows shows how to identify good sources of protein, carbohydrates and fat. Provided you vary your diet and don't eat the same menu every day, you need not be too concerned as to whether you are getting enough vitamins and minerals. The chances are that you will be, but it is important not to overcook foods, especially vegetables, as this will destroy vitamins. Vitamins B and C cannot be stored in the body, so to ensure you get enough make sure that every day you eat some foods containing them; for vitamin B go for bread and cereals, yeast extract, milk, cheese, eggs, lean meat and green vegetables; for vitamin C go for fruit, especially citrus, green vegetables, potatoes, salads and tomatoes.

Protein foods	Carbohydrate foods	Fats
Bread and flour	Bread and flour	Cheese
Cereals (of all kinds, including breakfast, rice, bulgar wheat etc.)	Cereals (of all kinds, including breakfast, rice, bulgar wheat etc.)	Egg yolk
		Fish
		Margarine & spreads (sunflower, soya, olive)
Cheese (especially low fat cheeses like cottage and curd cheeses)	Fruit (fresh, dried and juices)	Meat
	Honey	Milk
Eggs (maximum 5 a week)	Pasta	Nuts
Fish (2 or 3 times a week)	Pastries, biscuits, cakes (made with wholemeal flour, oatmeal, nuts, dried fruits, vegetable oils	Oils (polyunsaturated)
Meat (lean)		Poultry and game
Milk (semi-skimmed and low fat)		Yogurt (plain, low fat, Bio)

(contd over)

Protein foods	Carbohydrate foods	Fats
Nuts	e.g. flapjacks,digestive	
Pasta	biscuits, banana bread etc.)	
Peas (fresh or frozen)	Peas (fresh or frozen)	
Potatoes	Potatoes	
Poultry and game	Pulses (i.e. dried beans)	
Pulses (i.e. dried beans)	Vegetables (fresh, dried,	
Yogurt (plain, low fat, Bio)	frozen and canned)	
	Yogurt (plain, low	
	fat, Bio)	

The following table illustrates foods you should treat as indulgences rather than part of your daily intake because they contain high amounts of animal fats, sugar or salt, all of which are today's bogey-men!

Anything fried in deep fat
or containing monosodium glutamate

Bought biscuits, pies, cakes and puddings

Bought meat pies, sausages rolls etc.

Canned meats and pies

Canned fruit

Cream

Drinks, canned, fizzy and sweetened

Fatty meat

Fats such as butter, lard, dripping,
margarines containing animal fats

High-fat cheeses and milk

Ice cream

Potato crisps

Smoked fish and meats

Sugar, sugar-coated cereals

Sweets and confectionery

Equipment

You may be lucky and find yourself living somewhere with a fully equipped kitchen but most students have to make do with quite basic facilities, which means you will have to buy certain items yourself. Of course if money was no object you could get everything you needed from the huge range of kitchen equipment sold in supermarkets, department stores and specialist shops. A better bet is to haunt local car-boot sales, charity shops and jumble sales, which is not only fun but also a quick way of collecting everything you need for very little outlay. Different people have different ideas, so the list below is only a guide as to what I think you would find useful. However, in order even to begin cooking, you will need a few essentials and these are listed first. As to the others, buy them gradually as and when you need them.

Essentials

- *Bottle opener and corkscrew*
- *Cheese grater*
- *Crockery* – 1 small and 1 large plate, a bowl for cereal etc. and a 300 ml ($\frac{1}{2}$ pint) mug which can double as a measure.
- *Colander or sieve* – for straining vegetables, pasta, the contents of cans etc.
- *Cutlery* – 1 knife, spoon, fork and teaspoon.
- *Frying pan* – an 18 cm (7 in) non-stick pan would be ideal for one person but don't use metal implements or scouring pads or powders as they will damage the surface.
- *Knife* – a really sharp kitchen one.
- *Saucepans* – two or three ranging in size from 1 to 3 litres (2–6 pints). Non-stick or enamel-coated are easy to clean and heavy-based pans are less likely to burn.
- *Set of cook's measuring spoons* – all spoon measurements in this book are based on standard sizes; 1 teaspoon is 5 ml; 1 dessert-

spoon is 10 ml; 1 tablespoon is 15 ml.
- *Spatula or fish slice* – made of non-stick material.
- *Tin opener*
- *Wooden spoon and fork* – more effective than metal for stirring pots and pans.
- *Wok* – for stir-frying vegetables and making quick dishes. Go for one at least 38 cm (15 in) diameter, because even when cooking only small quantities of food, the curved shape of the base ensures the food uses minimum oil and maximum heat; if cooking large amounts you need the space to toss the food. Buy it if you can from a Chinese shop because the price will be much lower than at specialist kitchen shops.

Useful equipment

Below are listed items of cooking equipment which you will find useful to add gradually to your arsenal. With luck you'll find you can share some of them with fellow students.

- *Baking sheet* – useful for cooking pizzas, pastry dishes, foil parcels etc.
- *Bowls* – 1 large for mixing and one pudding basin.
- *Casserole* – useful for making stews and it can double as a saucepan. Can be earthenware or metal. Enamelled cast-iron is ideal but very expensive, well worth looking out for at car-boot sales or in charity shops.
- *Chopping board* – wooden or melamine.
- *Cling film, foil, greaseproof paper, kitchen paper roll*
- *Egg whisk* – you can manage with a fork but a balloon-shaped wire whisk speeds the process.
- *Flan tin* or *ring* – 18 cm (7 in) diameter for pizzas, quiches etc.
- *Gratin dish* – a shallow dish made in earthenware, heat proof glass or tin for baking.
- *Grill pan with grid*
- *Insulated flask* – one with a wide mouth for making yogurt or

keeping soup hot for a packed lunch.

- *Loaf tin* – 1 litre (2 pint) size for gratins, meat and vegetable loaves etc.
- *Measuring jug* – one that gives solid and liquid measurements.
- *Mouli-légumes* – a gadget with three blades for grating, mashing and shredding. Especially useful for puréeing soups.
- *Potato baker* or *skewers* – on which to impale baking potatoes and so reduce the cooking time by about 15 minutes.
- *Potato masher*
- *Roasting tin*
- *Rolling pin* – if desperate, use a bottle.
- *Rubber scraper* – for scraping those last morsels out of a pan or bowl.
- *Steamer* – collapsible metal steamer which fits into a saucepan and allows you to use the pan to cook two or more things at once.
- *Teapot* – saves on the tea bags if you're always having friends around.
- *Vegetable peeler* – handy for peeling vegetables really thinly and more effective than using a knife. Can also be used for slicing cheese. Look out for the swivel-bladed variety; once you've mastered the technique of peeling away from yourself with quick, light strokes, you'll find it a great aid.

Present list

There are other more expensive items which you might find useful, although none of them is essential for the recipes in this book. However, they are worth considering in the unlikely event of your running out of ideas for your Christmas or birthday list!

- *Electric hand-held blender* – these are far cheaper than most table top models, prices start at around £15. They are simple to use, take up little space and are very easy to clean. They do a multitude of cooking chores including puréeing, mixing, beating and blending.

- *Electric kettle* – will save time and fuel as you can boil very small quantities and is especially useful if your cooking facilities are limited.
- *Electric multi-cooker* – a godsend for those with very limited cooking facilities, as it will fry, grill, roast and bake.
- *Electric sandwich maker* – great for quick snacks but beware, you'll have a queue of friends around.
- *Electric slow-cooker* – cooks at a very low temperature and is therefore cheap on electricity. Can be used for soups, stews, vegetables, even cakes and puddings. However, the cooking process takes up to 10 hours, so it is only for those who like to plan ahead.
- *Electric toaster*

Shopping choice

Whether you shop as and when you need something or prefer to buy things on a weekly basis will depend on your time, temperament and how much room there is in your kitchen to store things. Below are some notes on the different types of shops you can use.

Shopping

- *Supermarkets* – most are run very efficiently, so the food is usually fresh and competitively priced and just about everything you want is under one roof. Once familiar with the layout, you can shop speedily, make your own choices and you will find help or advice is usually readily obtainable. Their *own brands* are often good value and, because supermarkets can buy in huge quantities, branded goods are often much cheaper than elsewhere. You can sometimes find bargains as goods are reduced when they near their sell-by dates.
- *Small shops* – their great advantage is that they are often just around the corner and are open at all hours. Their prices are higher than supermarkets but the owners are usually friendly and helpful and a good butcher, fishmonger or greengrocer is worth cultivating. A helpful fishmonger especially is an absolute bonus as he/she will not only advise you what to buy and how to cook it but will clean, skin and bone a fish when asked.
- *Markets* – worth visiting, especially for local produce such as vegetables, fruit, fish, eggs etc. Watch out though that you are not being palmed off with bruised or damaged items and be especially careful about freshness when buying meat or fish. Bargains are often to be had at the end of the day.
- *Ethnic shops* – often good value for buying rice and grains, nuts, pulses, dried fruits etc.
- *Health shops* – useful sources for vegetarian ingredients, nut butters, grains, pulses, nuts, seeds, herb teas etc.

Buying and storing

If you are not used to food shopping, the choice available can be bewildering and, once having made your choice, it is not always easy to know how to store and keep things fresh.

Whenever possible store all things covered or wrapped, even if you are using a fridge because otherwise they become hard and dehydrated and strongly flavoured foods taint others. Uncovered food left exposed in a kitchen attracts not only dirt and flies but other delightful creatures like mice and cockroaches! It's worth saving plastic bags, containers and jars with lids to use as storage, as well as having a supply of cling film and foil.

The following list is a guide to some of the foods you might need.

- *Bacon* – should be pink, the fat white. Will keep, wrapped, in a fridge for up to 10 days. Eat within a day or two if you have no fridge. Streaky bacon, though cheap, has a high proportion of fat. Smoked bacon is quite salty, green or sweetcure bacon is milder.
- *Biscuits and cakes* -can be kept in airtight containers but don't mix the two as the biscuits will go soft.
- *Bottled sauces* – as well as obvious items like tomato ketchup and mayonnaise it's worth having a bottle of soy sauce on hand. Unfortunately the cheap ones are made from extract of beans and contain added colourings and are very inferior to the more expensive brands made from whole fermented beans. However, just a few drops will add greatly to the flavour of many dishes, so one bottle will last for ages. Made-up tomato sauces for pizzas and pasta are expensive and it's cheaper to make your own using a can of chopped tomatoes.
- *Bread* – keep, wrapped, either in the fridge or in a covered container or loosely wrapped in a plastic bag so the air can circulate. White bread is made from refined flour to which the miller adds nutrients, whereas wholemeal bread contains all the natural

nutrients as well as more fibre. Bread sold as *brown bread* is often made from white flour coloured brown. So it's worth checking labels.

- *Canned foods* – keep some in store for when you don't have time to shop, such as sardines, pilchards, tuna, baked beans and soups. Canned Italian tomatoes either whole or chopped are excellent value. Canned sauces are expensive: cheaper and as useful are condensed soups which can be used undiluted as a sauce with things like pasta, pancakes etc.
- *Cheese* – keep wrapped in a cool place. If kept in the fridge, remove it 30 minutes before using to develop its flavour. For cooking use hard varieties like Cheddar. Dry, left-over cheese can be grated and will keep several days in an airtight jar.
- *Coffee* – freeze-dried instant, though expensive, is more like the real thing. Like fresh coffee it doesn't have a long shelf-life so buy large jars only if you drink a lot. Ground coffee is very expensive so buy it in small quantities and keep in an airtight container, as it loses its aroma within a very short time. It can be stored in the fridge or even frozen.
- *Eggs* – store eggs at room temperature rather than the fridge; they will keep up to two weeks.
- *Fats* – cheapest fats for spreading are margarines and low fat spreads. Butter has the best flavour but is more expensive. Use oils rather than lard or dripping, which are both high in animal fats. Pastry can be made with special white fats sold for baking, though margarine or butter can be used. Fats will keep in the fridge for up to 1 month.
- *Fish* – can be stored, wrapped, in a fridge for 24 hours. If you have no fridge, eat the same day. Buy fish that looks firm and bright, avoid any which look dull and limp. There should be hardly any smell. Whole fish should have shiny eyes and red gills. Ask the fishmonger to gut and clean them for you (this involves removing the innards, any spiky fins and the scales). However, all pre-packed fish is sold ready to cook, as is frozen fish. Frozen fish

fillets or steaks can be cooked from frozen but whole fish needs to be completely defrosted first. Instructions will be on packets.

- *Flour* – buy in small quantities unless you plan to do lots of baking, and store in an airtight container. Plain flour is most often needed so if a recipe calls for self-raising, just add 1 teaspoon baking powder to every 150 g (6 oz, 1 mug) plain flour.
- *Fruit* – keep in a cool place. Don't refrigerate bananas as they turn black, or melons or pineapples as they absorb the flavours of other foods. Buy fruit which looks fresh and shiny and has no blemishes.
- *Herbs* and *spices* – do wonders for the simplest dish. They're not cheap, so begin with a jar of mixed dried herbs and then gradually buy others as you need them. If a recipe calls for a particular herb, you can often substitute another; the taste will be different but it can be just as delicious. You can grow fresh herbs in pots on a window-sill and might be able to obtain cuttings from a gardening friend. As for spices, the first to go for are black peppercorns which you grind in a pepper-mill; the flavour is infinitely more subtle than the powdered variety and good cooks swear by them. Otherwise collect spices as and when.
- *Lemon juice* – lemons give zest to many dishes especially fish, but they're expensive, so look out for the juice sold in plastic lemons. One of these will last for ages.
- *Meat* – provides a lot of protein but can be expensive. Fortunately, there's the same amount of protein in cheaper cuts, although those that contain a lot of fat are not necessarily a good buy, as, by the time you've discarded the fat, not much may be left that is edible. Choose meat which looks moist rather than wet, is firm and elastic to touch and has very little smell. Beef should be dark red with firm, yellow fat. Lamb should be dull red with hard, white fat. Pork should be pale pink with soft, white fat. Bacteria can multiply rapidly in meat so certain rules have to be followed. Without a fridge eat the day you buy. If using a fridge, store meat at the top where it is coolest but make sure

none of the juices leak onto other food which could cause cross-infection. Store mince or offal (liver, kidneys etc.) for no longer than 24 hours and bought, cooked meats within 2 days of purchase. Other meat will keep up to 4 days but, if it is pre-packed before refrigerating, remove the packaging and put the meat into a plastic bag loosely tied. Always make sure frozen meat is completely thawed before cooking and there are no ice particles lurking and never refreeze it once it has thawed. The thawing process can be hastened by standing the meat under cold, running water, never the hot tap. Casseroles prepared one day to be eaten the next must be cooled down before they go in the fridge, then reheated to boiling point the next day and simmered for 15–20 minutes.

- *Milk* – keep in a dark, cool place because light will destroy the vitamins. Low fat contains just as many nutrients, sometimes more, than high fat varieties. Long-life or UHT milk is a good store standby although some people don't like the taste, especially in tea, but it is very good for making yogurt as it is already boiled. Skimmed powdered milk is useful for making up milk in an emergency or adding to home-made yogurt.

- *Mixes* – mixes for making pizza bases, mashed potato and pastry are useful to have on hand.

- *Oil* – go for polyunsaturated kinds which include corn, sunflower, soya or groundnut. Avoid brands labelled *cooking oil* which although cheaper often have a fishy flavour and the money saved is minimal.

- *Pasta* – there's a huge variety. The dried keeps for ages whereas the fresh must be eaten right away. Always have at least some long spaghetti to hand.

- *Pesto* – delicious basil flavoured sauce from Italy sold in jars. It has a strong flavour so, although expensive, a little goes a long way.

- *Pulses* – can be the base of many substantial meals. Some need long soaking before they are cooked, so if you want to save time it's worth considering the many excellent canned varieties. These include aduki beans, black beans, butter beans, cannellini beans, chickpeas, haricot beans, red kidney beans and soya beans. Some pulses, notably lentils, dried peas, mung beans and blackeyed beans, need no soaking so are worth buying dried.

- *Rice and grains* – go for long-grained or Patna rice, sometimes labelled American rice. Quick-cook rices are more expensive and don't really save any effort. Brown rice contains more nutrients and has a distinct nutty flavour but it takes twice as long to cook as white rice. Other grains to go for include bulgar wheat, millet, buckwheat and couscous.
- *Sun-dried tomatoes* – very fashionable, perhaps because they are so delicious. Have an intense flavour and can be used sparingly so, although pricey, a jar can last for ages.
- *Stock cubes* – will give flavour to soups and stews and can be used in recipes which call for stock (flavoured liquid made from bones or vegetables, recipe on page 46). Different flavours are available including chicken, beef, fish and vegetable.
- *Tea* – loose tea is cheaper though less convenient than bags.
- *Tomato purée* – adds flavour to all sorts of dishes. Sold in cans, jars and tubes, the latter perhaps being the most practical.
- *Tomatoes, canned* – excellent for many recipes which call for tomatoes because the flavour is so good and they are cheap. Go for the Italian variety and lean towards the chopped ones, they save time but also are far less watery than the whole ones.
- *Vegetables* – keep in a cool, dark place, especially potatoes which go green and become toxic if kept in the light. Green vegetables should be eaten as soon as possible. Root vegetables will keep for about 1 week but don't store them in plastic bags out of the fridge or they will begin to sweat and ferment. Salads should be kept, loosely wrapped, in plastic bags at the bottom of the fridge. If using only half a root vegetable, retain the root end until last because the cut piece will draw nourishment from it and remain fresh longer.
- *Vinegar* – use wine or cider vinegars for salad dressings and in the

recipes. Malt is far too strong except for sprinkling on fish and chips or making pickles.

- *Yogurt* – keeps for several days in the fridge. Go for natural, plain yogurts; Bio is best. Greek style yogurts are thick and creamy and especially delicious if made from ewe's or goat's milk. Many commercial yogurts look mouthwateringly tempting but most contain artificial sweeteners and flavourings and it's much cheaper to add your own fruit, nuts, honey etc. to plain yogurt. It's easy too to make your own and by far the cheapest option (see page 133).

Quantities, measurements and temperatures

- *Quantities* – the recipes in this book are for 1 person unless otherwise stated. If increasing quantities for more than one, be careful about additional seasoning. You won't need twice as much salt, for example, when preparing for two. So taste as you go. Appetites vary, so you may find you need to prepare a little more or less than I have suggested.
- *Measurements* – officially we have gone metric but old habits die hard and inevitably some things will still be sold using the imperial measurements. For this reason measurements in this book are given in both metric and imperial amounts. They don't translate comfortably, for example 1 ounce is 28.3 grams, so, to make life easier, the amounts are rounded up or down to give an approximate value. This means that, when using the recipes, you should go for either metric or imperial and not mix the two together. Because most students won't have a set of scales or even a liquid measure, I have also given amounts in the recipes using mugs and spoons. The mug is based on one measuring approximately 300 ml ($\frac{1}{2}$ pint) and the spoons are based on a standard set of cook's measuring spoons which are marked in millilitres: 1 teaspoon being 5 ml, 1 dessertspoon being 10 ml and 1 tablespoon being 15 ml. Don't be too alarmed by all of this. You'll find that absolutely precise measurements aren't too critical for most things. The only time you need to be especially careful is if you make things like bread or cakes.

Below is a table which converts some spoon and mug measures into ounces and grams. If you have no other means of measuring, you might find it useful if you want to use recipes from other sources.

Spoon and mug conversions

Honey	1 tablespoon =	a 300 ml ($\frac{1}{2}$ pint) mug =
Jam	1 oz or	10 oz or
Syrup	25 grams approx.	275 grams approx.
Treacle		
Fats	2 tablespoons =	a 300 ml ($\frac{1}{2}$ pint) mug =
Oil	1 oz or	8 oz or
Rice	25 grams approx.	225 grams approx.
Sugar		
Cocoa	3 tablespoons =	a 300 ml ($\frac{1}{2}$ pint) mug =
Cornflour	1 oz or	6 oz or
Flour	25 grams approx.	150 grams approx.
Breadcrumbs	4 tablespoons =	a 300 ml ($\frac{1}{2}$ pint) mug =
Cheese, grated	1 oz or	4 oz or
Oats	25 grams approx.	100 grams approx.

- **Liquid measures**
  1 pint = 20 fluid ounces
  1 litre = 35 fluid ounces
  $1\frac{3}{4}$ pints = 1 litre
- **Weights**
  1 pound = 450 grams approx.
  1 kilogram = 2.2 pounds
- **Oven temperatures** – an electric oven needs to be preheated for about 10 minutes before you begin to cook. Food can be put straight into a gas oven from cold but then you need to increase the cooking times given in the recipes by about 10 minutes. Ovens do vary, so you may have to modify the times given slightly. Cultivate your nose! Your sense of smell is a reliable guide to when something is cooked or when it is beginning to burn.

Oven temperatures are given for gas regulo marks, electric Fahrenheit and Celsius (or centigrade). Below is a conversion chart which might come in handy.

	Gas	°Fahrenheit	°Celsius (centigrade)
Very low	¼	225	110
	½	250	120
Low	1	275	140
	2	300	150
Moderate	3	325	160
	4	350	180
Moderately hot	5	375	190
	6	400	200
Hot	7	425	220
	8	450	230
Very hot	9	475	240

• *Some notes on using a cooker* – if you're new to cooking, you may not know that it is cheaper to use the top of the stove rather than the grill, and that it is more expensive than either to use the oven. So if possible use the oven only when you have more than one thing to cook, or share the oven space with someone else who's cooking at the same time. However, it's probably cheaper to be using the oven to cook a couple of jacket potatoes, say, than it would be to get a take-away!

You can save money on gas or electricity by always covering pans when you're bringing things to the boil and by putting only as much water as you need into your kettle.

Breakfasts and anytime snacks

No-cook start

One thing is for sure, you're always hungry, so whether it's just breakfast or an anytime snack, you'll often feel the need for something reasonably instant. Perhaps you're lucky and have a canteen which provides cheap bites, but, whether you have or not, it's obviously cheaper still to make your own. They needn't be complicated and they needn't necessarily involve any cooking at all. The simplest might be a cup of tea or coffee or perhaps a glass of milk or fruit juice with a bowl of cereal and, if there's time, a couple of pieces of toast and your favourite spread. For days when you're really hard pressed you could always grab a carton of yogurt and a piece of fruit and eat them with a hunk of bread or even a flapjack or a slice of banana bread (recipes on pages 161–2).

Cereals

Almost any kind of cereal will provide you with a quick fillip but it can be made more interesting by adding fruit, either fresh or dried and perhaps a spoonful of honey instead of sugar. It takes only a few minutes to peel and slice a banana or kiwi fruit or chop up an apple or pear. As for dried fruits, there's a huge variety on sale, including currants, raisins and sultanas, chopped dates, peaches and prunes. Especially nice are dried apricots. Look out for shrivelled brown apricots in ethnic shops, often much cheaper than the supermarket or health food kind. They look like gnarled walnuts but cover them in boiling water, leave them to soak and swell overnight and they will double their size and taste as sweet as caramelized sugar.

Muesli

From the point of view of food value, muesli is probably the best cereal choice. It was invented by a Swiss, Dr Bircher-Benner, originally as a light and nourishing supper dish, the cereal, fruit, nuts and yogurt providing a complete meal. It's widely available from supermarkets, health and small food shops. *Own brands* are often cheaper. Cheaper still is to mix your own. The following quantities are only a guide and will provide one serving. You might think it worthwhile making up a much larger quantity and storing it in an airtight container. Vary the proportions as you will and experiment with different grains, fruit and nuts. The fruit you add can be almost anything from apples, bananas, pears or plums to more exotic fruits like kiwis or when they are in season strawberries, raspberries, cherries, peaches or apricots.

2 tablespoons oatmeal
2 tablespoons wheat flakes
$1/2$ tablespoon wheatgerm, optional
$1/2$ tablespoon chopped mixed nuts
1 tablespoon dried fruit
milk or fruit juice
sliced fruit
2 or 3 tablespoons yogurt

Mix the oatmeal, wheat flakes, wheatgerm, nuts and dried fruit together. Pour in the milk or fruit juice. Top with the sliced fruit and the yogurt.

Easy cook

Porridge

Porridge is the almost instant hot breakfast or snack, especially if you make it using the packaged variety, which entails nothing more than adding hot milk or water to the cereal and giving it a stir. Follow directions on the packet. Eat it with sugar and honey or jam and a helping of cold milk. A pinch of nutmeg or cinnamon adds greatly to the flavour.

Alternatively you can make the real thing by buying rolled oats, which is refined oatmeal and usually sold as *porridge oats*, again instructions are on the packet. Although cheaper than the instant variety, it takes slightly longer to make as the oats have to be cooked and stirred for 4–5 minutes to prevent the porridge burning.

Cheapest of all is to use unrefined oatmeal which is soaked overnight in cold water, then simmered for 5–10 minutes, before being brought to the boil and stirred on a very low heat for 5–10 minutes.

Eggs, boiled and coddled

An egg provides a cheap and nutritional snack and boiled and coddled eggs are the easiest to do. Eat them with soldiers of toast and recover your childhood! An egg taken straight from the fridge tends to crack when boiled; to prevent this, try piercing a hole in one end with a needle.

To boil an egg
1 egg

Put the egg into a small saucepan and just cover with cold water. Bring to the boil and as soon as the water begins to bubble start timing:

Runny – 3½ minutes
Firm white and runny yolk – 4 minutes

Firm white and yolk – 5 minutes
Hardboiled – 9 minutes

To coddle an egg

Half fill a pan with water, bring to the boil and add the egg (preferably not straight from the fridge, if so pierce with a needle). Remove the pan immediately from the heat, cover and leave for 5 minutes before eating.

Banana and bacon

A simple treat on a cold morning.

1 banana
2 rashers of streaky bacon
1/2 tablespoon of oil, margarine or butter

Cut the banana in half round its middle and wrap each half in a rasher of bacon. Heat the oil, margarine or butter in a frying pan and, when it is foaming, add the wrapped banana halves. Fry gently, turning them over once or twice, until the bacon is crisp and the banana soft, about 3–5 minutes.

Fried eggs and tomatoes

This is a recipe from Provence. Tomatoes flavoured with garlic are cooked until they are meltingly soft before the eggs are broken on top and cooked until they are just set.

2 tablespoons oil
2 or 3 tomatoes, quartered
1 clove garlic cut in two
1/2 teaspoon dried mixed herbs
2 eggs

Heat the oil in a frying pan and add the tomatoes, garlic and herbs. Let them cook gently until they are very soft, 15–20 minutes. Break in the eggs and continue to cook until they are set.

Sandwiches

A sandwich is not just a clever way of enclosing and keeping food fresh, it also provides a simple but well-balanced meal. Use ordinary bread or experiment with all sorts of other breads. You can add fillings to rolls or baps as well as more unusual breads like pitta and Naan, or you could use a French baguette sliced lengthwise or an Italian bread like ciabatta. To complete your snack, drink a carton of fresh fruit juice or some milk or eat a carton of yogurt.

Don't always spread your sandwiches with margarine or butter but ring the changes by using one of the following: mayonnaise, a soft cheese like curd, cream or cottage, or a butter like peanut or tahini (tahini butter which is made from sesame seeds is sold in health shops).

If you want to be organized, sandwiches can be made the night before and kept in the fridge in a plastic bag or wrapped in foil. Or if you like to really plan ahead, they can be frozen. They take 3–4 hours to thaw but must not contain mayonnaise, salad creams, salad ingredients, hard-boiled eggs or bananas, none of which freeze well.

You'll already have your own ideas as to the perfect sandwich but here are some others to help you.

Sandwich fillings

- *Bacon* – fried or grilled, made while the bacon is still warm and topped with lettuce.
- *Banana* – with one of the following: lemon juice; a nut butter like peanut or tahini; chocolate spread or jam; honey alone or with raisins; a slice of ham.
- *Cheddar* – or similar cheese with one of the following: chutney; chopped dates, nuts or pineapple (canned); sliced tomato, mushrooms or cucumber; yeast extract; raisins.
- *Cottage, curd* or *cream cheese* – with one of the following: sliced

tomato, cucumber or banana; mashed sardines or pilchards; chopped dates or orange.

- *Egg* – either hard-boiled egg or mumbled (see p. 31) with one of the following: peanut butter; yeast extract; lettuce.
- *Fish* – canned, such as tuna, sardines, pilchards with a topping of lettuce, sliced tomato or cucumber.
- *Meat* – cold, sliced, spread with mustard and topped with lettuce, sliced tomato or cucumber; or chutney or pickles.
- *Sweetcorn* – (canned) with mayonnaise or chutney.

Things on toast

It doesn't matter what time of the day or night it is, something on toast could be the answer. Of course, the easiest things to serve on toast are out of a can. Everyone knows baked beans, which are not to be despised because they are full of goodness. They are great on their own or topped with a poached egg. Sardines, mackerel and pilchards too are both cheap and tasty and made even more so if a little mustard is spread on the toast, or you could try them sprinkled with a few drops of lemon juice, Worcester sauce, tomato ketchup or vinegar.

Cinnamon toast

This is a treat that belongs to students. It used to be made in Oxford by the college scouts, perhaps it still is. Whatever the case, it is simple enough to make yourself.

Slices of bread toasted on one side only
butter
sugar
powdered cinnamon

Spread the toasted bread with butter, sprinkle with a little sugar and cinnamon and put under the hot grill until sugar and cinnamon melt into each other.

Tomatoes on toast

1–2 slices buttered toast
1 tablespoon oil
2 or 3 tomatoes, cut in half
salt and pepper

Either fry the tomatoes by heating the oil in a frying pan, adding the tomatoes skin side down and turning them once until soft, *or* put them in a grill pan, sprinkle with oil and put under a hot grill. Pile them on the toast and season with salt and pepper.

Mushrooms on toast

Fried or grilled mushrooms are delicious flavoured with a finely chopped clove of garlic and a sprinkling of mixed herbs. They go well too with bacon either grilled or finely chopped and fried with the mushrooms.

100 g (4 oz) mushrooms
1 tablespoon oil
salt and pepper

Wipe the mushrooms to remove the dirt. Either fry them by heating the oil and turning them over once or twice until they are hot through, or put them under a hot grill sprinkled with oil. Season with salt and pepper.

Bruschetta

If you like garlic, then this is for you. It's the Italian version of toast, which can be made by grilling or baking slices of bread (buy ciabatta if you can) at the top of a hot oven, Gas 7/425°F/220°C for 10 minutes. It is then rubbed with garlic and sprinkled with a little oil. Eat it with any sort of topping from crushed sardines or anchovies to sun-dried tomatoes or perhaps a spread of pesto. Spread the toasted bread with your topping and put back under the grill or into the oven until hot through.

Cheese on toast

English cheeses are particularly good for cooking. Go for one of the hard varieties like Cheddar, Red Leicester, Wensleydale or Cheshire but whatever you choose, take care not to overcook it, or it will become stringy and indigestible.

50 g cheese, sliced or grated
buttered toast

Heat the grill for a few minutes. Slice the cheese and lay it on the toast, put under the grill until the cheese melts and bubbles.
Ring the changes by putting one of the following under the cheese before grilling:

- a slice of ham
- a sliced tomato
- yeast extract
- grilled bacon
- sliced banana
- beansprouts
- sliced mushrooms

Goat's cheese on toasted French bread

Goat's cheese melts to a creamy mass and makes a delicious snack. If you can't get it, you could use curd cheese instead. If you like garlic, cut a clove in half and rub the cut sides all over the slices of bread before you toast them.

2 x 2 cm (1 in) thick slices French bread
oil
100 g (4 oz) goat's cheese

Heat the grill. Sprinkle the bread with oil and put it under the grill until it begins to turn golden. Cover with slices of goat's cheese and put back under the grill until it melts and bubbles.

Welsh rarebit

Delicious with a slice or two of grilled or fried bacon and even more so topped with a poached egg (see below), when it becomes *Buck rarebit*. For a variation try mixing the cheese with a little beer.

$1/4$ teaspoon made mustard
4 tablespoons cheese, grated
little milk
buttered toast

Mix the mustard and cheese and add just enough milk to form a thick paste. Spread it on the toast and put under the grill until bubbling and golden.

Poached egg

Poached eggs have a habit of becoming straggly, especially so if the eggs are more than a few days old. Your first attempt may be a bit discouraging but it's worth trying again, because once mastered, poaching is a quick and handy way of cooking eggs.

1 egg (or 2)
buttered toast

Half fill a frying pan with water. Bring it to the boil, lower the heat and pull the pan half off the burner, so that only half the water is simmering. Break the egg into the water (if you are nervous, break it on to a saucer and slide it into the water). Cover the pan and leave the egg to set, about 4 minutes. (Some electric burners are difficult to control, so if you find the water is bubbling too fiercely, remove the pan completely from the heat.) Remove the egg with a spatula and put on the toast.

As well as being good to eat on toast, with or without cheese or Welsh rarebit, poached egg is also good with spinach or smoked fish like haddock or kippers.

Double Gloucester cheese and ale – 2 servings

Double Gloucester is a good melting cheese and in this old English recipe it is combined with ale and toast to make a snack to impress your friends. It should be eaten with pickles and mulled ale. You could use Cheddar or Red Leicester instead.

100 g (4 oz) cheese, thinly sliced
$\frac{1}{2}$ teaspoon prepared mustard
4 tablespoons ale
2 slices toast

Heat the oven to Gas 5/375°F/190°C. Put the sliced cheese into a shallow oven-proof dish. Spread with the mustard and spoon over the ale. Put into the oven for 5–10 minutes until the cheese melts. Put the toast on plates and spoon over the cheese and ale mixture.

Fried egg on toast

1 tablespoon oil
1 egg (or 2)
buttered toast

Heat the oil in a frying pan, when it is hot, break in the egg and let it cook over a medium heat until the white is set. If you like the yolk covered with a cloudy skin, spoon some of the hot oil over it while it is cooking. Remove with a spatula and slide on to the toast.

Fried or grilled bacon

No one needs an introduction to fried or grilled bacon served with an egg! Fry the bacon rashers in a very little oil or put them under a hot grill, turning them over once or twice until they are as you like them.

Scrambled eggs on toast

Eat them on their own or for a change stir a tablespoon or two of cheese into the mixture. Or have them with grilled or fried tomatoes or mushrooms, see pages 26–27. Or top them with a sliced courgette which you have cooked gently in oil, margarine or butter for about 10 minutes and seasoned with salt and pepper and perhaps a pinch or two of mixed herbs.

2 eggs
1 dessertspoon milk
salt and pepper
1 tablespoon oil, margarine or butter
buttered toast

Break the eggs into a bowl, beat with a fork until mixed and frothy, stir in the milk and season with salt and pepper. Heat the oil, margarine or butter in a small saucepan over a low heat, pour in the eggs, stir gently until they thicken and are set and glistening but still a little runny. (Over-cooking makes them dry and stringy.) Pile on to the toast.

Mumbled eggs

An even easier version of scrambled eggs because the whole operation is done in the pan. Use the same ingredients as in the above recipe but omit the milk. Heat a frying pan over a low heat with the oil, margarine or butter. When it is foaming, break in the eggs and stir quickly to mix them. Keep stirring until they are set but still moist. Season to taste with the salt and pepper.

Soft herring roes

Very cheap and very delicious, especially if you sprinkle them with a few drops of lemon juice.

1 tablespoon oil or margarine
100 g soft herring roes
1 teaspoon made mustard
buttered toast

Heat the oil or margarine in a small pan, stir in the mustard and add the roes. Let them cook gently for 5–7 minutes, turning them once or twice until they are hot. Pile on to the toast.

Fried breads and hot sandwiches

If you have no grill or toaster, fry a piece of bread instead. The secret of crisp, non-greasy fried bread is really hot oil.

1–2 tablespoons oil
1 piece of bread

Heat a frying pan with the oil until it is really hot, add the bread and turn it over when the underside is golden. If all the oil has been absorbed, add a little more. Fry the other side and eat piping hot.

Pain perdu

This rather romantic name translated means nothing more romantic than *stale bread*. However, when mixed with beaten egg and fried, it becomes a quick and moreish snack especially if eaten with a generous dollop of jam, sugar, honey or syrup, and becomes even more delicious sprinkled with a little powdered nutmeg or cinnamon.

1 egg
2 tablespoons milk
2 slices stale bread
2 tablespoons oil or butter

Beat the egg with the milk on a plate. Dip the bread slices in it, coating both sides. Heat the oil, margarine or butter and when it is foaming quickly fry the bread, turning it once so that both sides are golden.

Poor Knights of Windsor

The same as *pain perdu*, but the two slices of bread are sandwiched together with a sweet filling before being dipped in the egg mixture and fried.

Savoury fried sandwich with egg

Make exactly as *Poor Knights of Windsor* but fill the sandwich with a savoury filling. (A delicious solution to what to do with those sandwiches you forgot to eat at lunchtime!)

Toasted sandwiches

Of course if you have an electric sandwich maker, toasting sandwiches is very easy. Even if you haven't, it still isn't difficult to make them.

2 slices bread
margarine or butter, optional
filling, see below

Toast the bread on one side only. Spread the toasted side with margarine or butter if using. Put filling between the slices and put back under the grill, turning once to toast both the other sides.

Fried sandwiches

2 slices bread spread with margarine or butter
filling, see below

Heat the frying pan, put in one slice of bread, fat side down, add filling. Top with the second slice, fat side up. Fry until the underside is golden, turn the sandwich over and fry the other side.

Suggested fillings
- *Bacon* – grilled or fried with sliced banana or tomato.
- *Baked beans* – a spoonful or two.
- *Banana* – mashed with lemon juice or honey.
- *Cheese* – like Cheddar, sliced or grated, or a soft cheese like cottage or curd, with one of the following, sliced tomato, mushrooms, or cooked potato; pickles or chutney; chopped orange or dates; sliced cold meat like ham or salami; yeast extract.
- *Egg* – fried or poached.

- *Fish* – (canned) like sardines, pilchards or tuna with or without sliced tomato.
- *Meat* – such as a slice or two of ham, chicken, salami or other Continental sausage.
- *Tomato* – sliced with peanut butter or sweetcorn (canned).

Potato snacks

Stuffed jacket potatoes

A stuffed jacket potato is a great anytime snack and because it is cooked in its skin it retains most of its food value as well as its flavour. It may seem extravagant to use the oven just to bake one potato, it's obviously less so if several of you are cooking together, but because the potato itself is relatively cheap, the extravagance can easily be justified. If you like your potatoes to have crisp skins, roll them in coarse salt before baking them but if you like the skins soft, wipe them over with a little oil.

1 large potato per person
choice of filling, see below

Heat the oven to Gas 7/425°F/220°C. Wash and dry the potatoes and cut a cross on top with a sharp knife or prick the skin all over with a fork (this allows steam to escape and prevents the potato bursting). To reduce the cooking time, spike the potato with a skewer, potato baker (sold in kitchen shops) or a stainless steel fork – the metal acts as a heat conductor. Bake until the potatoes are soft, 45–60 minutes.

Fillings

The cooked potatoes can be simply cut almost in half and filled with a generous knob of butter or margarine and a good sprinkling of salt and pepper with perhaps a dollop of grated or curd cheese, or a spoonful or two of yogurt; or you could fill them with salad ingredients mixed with a little mayonnaise, salad dressing or yogurt.

Or make a more elaborate filling by cutting the potatoes in half, scooping out most of the flesh and mixing it with one of the suggestions below. Pile the mixture back into the potato halves, top with either grated, cottage or curd cheese and return to the oven for 5–10 minutes until the filling is hot and the cheese melted and beginning to brown.

- *Bacon* – chop and fry 1 or 2 rashers with a sliced tomato, or two or three mushrooms or any combination of stir-fried vegetables, mix with a tablespoon of cottage or curd cheese.
- *Egg* – either mix up a beaten egg with the potato or instead of cutting the potato in half, slice off the top, scoop out sufficient potato flesh to take an egg. Break an egg into this hollow, top with grated cheese and return to the oven until the white is set but the yolk is still runny, about 10 minutes.
- *Fish* – mix a tablespoon or two of canned tuna, mashed sardines or pilchards with a little tomato ketchup.
- *Meat* – use cooked meat like ham or chicken, slice it finely and mix with a little mustard and yogurt or cottage or curd cheese.
- *Pulses* – a tablespoon or two of almost any kind of beans or sweetcorn.
- *Vegetables* – almost any combination of stir-fried vegetables (see page 69).

Fanned potatoes

For a change try fanned potatoes. Heat the oven to Gas 7/425°F/220°C. Slice large potatoes at 5 mm ($^1/_4$ in) intervals almost to the base so that the potatoes still hold together. Put on to a baking sheet and sprinkle with oil, salt and pepper. Bake for 45–60 minutes. 10 minutes before they are ready, sprinkle them with more oil, a chopped clove of garlic and herbs of your choice.

Panhaggerty

This dish, the name of which means onions and potatoes, comes from Northumberland where it is traditionally cooked in beef dripping but in our diet conscious age, oil is the preferred medium. It makes a filling and tasty snack.

2 tablespoons of oil
225 g (8 oz) potatoes, peeled and thinly sliced
1 medium onion, peeled and thinly sliced

4 tablespoons grated cheese such as Cheddar
pepper and salt

Heat the oil in a small frying pan and lay the potatoes over the base. Top with the onions and sprinkle with the grated cheese. Season with salt and pepper. Cover with a piece of kitchen foil and put on a lid. Fry over a low heat for about 40 minutes until the vegetables are cooked. Heat the grill until very hot and put the pan under it until the top is golden brown.

Single-pan cooking

Soups
Omelettes
Pizzas
Pulses mean beans
Parcels
Fish
Stir-fry
Grilled meats and hamburgers

Soups

Of course you can just open a can, heat it through and eat but once you have made and tasted home-made soup, you'll discover it is worth the small amount of trouble. And what's more, it's cheap. A perfect single-pan meal especially if eaten with a hunk of bread or buttered toast.

Other accompaniments to soup are:

- *Bacon* – add a fried chopped rasher or two of bacon.
- *Cheese* – sprinkle over two or three tablespoons grated cheese.
- *Croutons* – fry small cubes of bread in hot oil until golden.
- *Garlic or herb bread* – Sprinkle slices of bread with chopped garlic or dried herbs and a smattering of oil. Crisp them either under the grill, in a frying pan or at the top of a hot oven.

Soups can be made more filling by throwing in a handful of rice, small pasta, dried red lentils or split peas once the liquid has been added and brought to the boil. Or you could follow the French peasant's example, which is to break an egg or two carefully on top of the cooked soup, put on the lid and leave it to poach gently for 3 or 4 minutes. The combination of soup and egg is delicious.

The recipes below are for more than one serving but soup will keep for several days if refrigerated and reheats in minutes.

Vegetable soup

There are dozens of recipes for vegetable soups but most of them follow the same basic method given below. (Instead of plain water, you can use the water in which vegetables have been cooked, which not only adds to the flavour but also increases the nutritional value. Or you can make your own stock by using the bones from a chicken carcass, see page 46).

2 tablespoons oil
1 onion, chopped

450 g (1 lb) vegetables, finely chopped or sliced – see below for
    suggestions
1 litre (1³⁄₄ pints, 4 mugs) stock (or water flavoured with either 1
    stock cube, crumbled or 1 teaspoon soy sauce or 1 tablespoon
    tomato purée or 1 tablespoon pesto)
salt and pepper

Heat the oil in a large saucepan and add the chopped onion and
other vegetables. Stir them well, lower the heat, put on the lid and
leave them to sweat for 10 minutes to release their flavours. Pour in
the stock or flavoured water and season with ¹⁄₂ teaspoon salt and
a sprinkling of pepper. Raise the heat, cover the pan and bring to
the boil. When it boils, lower the heat and let it simmer for about
30 minutes.

Serve as it is or if you like, crush the vegetables using a potato-
masher or, if you happen to have a sieve, Mouli-légumes or an electric hand-held blender you can reduce the soup to a purée.

Suggested vegetables to use

The following are suggestions but don't be afraid of improvising
your own mixtures and remember, if you have herbs on hand, a
sprinkle of either fresh or dried will add to the flavour and, if you
like garlic, add a clove or two finely chopped.

All vegetables must be washed and chopped or sliced but they
don't all need peeling, as even potatoes and carrots can be cooked
in their skins.

- *Carrots and peas* – 350 g (12 oz) carrots and 100 g (4 oz) frozen
  peas, these last to be added a few minutes before the soup is cooked.
- *Carrots and onions* – 225 g (8 oz) of each.
- *Carrots and potatoes* – 225 g (8 oz) of each.
- *Carrots, potatoes and leeks* – in equal quantities.
- *Leek and potato* – 225 g (8 oz) of each but omit the onion.
- *Leek, tomato and sweet pepper* – 2 leeks, 2 tomatoes and a red or
  green pepper.

- *Parsnip and apple* – 350 g (12 oz) parsnips and 2 crisp eating apples.
- *Spinach and potato* – 225 g (8 oz) of each. (Spinach should be well washed because it can be gritty. Try this soup flavoured with a pinch of nutmeg and with a spoonful of yogurt stirred in.)
- *Watercress and potato* – 1 bunch of watercress and 225 g (8 oz) potatoes.

Split pea soup

This soup, nicknamed *London Particular* after Dickens's description of a pea soup fog, is thick and rich and immensely filling. It is made with bacon and yellow split peas.

2 rashers streaky bacon, chopped
1 onion, chopped
1 carrot, chopped
225 g (8 oz) split peas
1 litre (1¾ pints) stock *or* water + 1 stock cube
salt and pepper

Put the chopped bacon into a saucepan and cook it over a low heat until the fat runs out. Add the onion and carrot and stir them over a low heat for a few minutes. Pour in the liquid, add the split peas and crumble in the stock cube. Add ½ teaspoon salt and a sprinkling of pepper. Bring the soup to the boil, cover and simmer it over a low heat until the peas are tender, about 45 minutes.

Kettle broth

This Cornish bacon and leek soup gets its name from the kettle in which it was cooked which was in fact an iron cauldron suspended over the fire. What makes it special is that it is flavoured and coloured with marigold petals. If there aren't any growing round you, use tomato purée instead.

2 tablespoons oil
450 g (1 lb) leeks, cleaned and sliced
4 rashers streaky bacon, chopped
600 ml (1 pint) stock *or* water + 1 chicken stock cube
salt and pepper
2 or 3 marigolds or 1 tablespoon tomato purée

Heat the oil in a large saucepan and add the leeks and bacon. Cover the pan and leave over a low heat for 10 minutes. Crumble in the stock cube, add the liquid and bring to the boil. Add $\frac{1}{2}$ teaspoon salt and a sprinkling of pepper and the petals from the marigolds or the tomato purée. Put on a low heat and simmer, covered, for 30 minutes.

French onion soup

This French peasant soup became famous in the *bistros* of Paris. It is heartwarming on a bleak winter's night.

900 g (2 lbs) onions
2 tablespoons oil
1 teaspoon sugar
1 litre (1$\frac{3}{4}$ pints, 3 mugs) stock *or* water + 1 stock cube
salt and pepper
one slice of toast per person
slices of cheese to cover

Peel and slice the onions. Heat the oil in a large pan, add the onions and sugar and cook over a medium heat until they are soft and brown, 15–20 minutes, turning the slices over from time to time. Pour in the liquid, crumble in the stock cube, bring to the boil, cover and simmer on a low heat for 15 minutes. Season to taste with salt and pepper.

Put slices of cheese on to slices of toast and put under the grill until the cheese melts and bubbles. Float a piece of toast on top of each serving of soup.

Sweetcorn soup

1 tablespoon oil
1 onion, chopped
2 potatoes, chopped
225 g (8 oz) water
600 ml (1 pint) milk
salt and pepper
medium can of sweetcorn

Heat the oil in a large saucepan, add the chopped onion and potatoes and cook over a low heat, covered, for 5–10 minutes. Add the water and milk, $\frac{1}{2}$ teaspoon salt and a sprinkling of pepper. Bring to the boil and add the sweetcorn. Cover and simmer for 20 minutes over a low heat.

Chickpea and tomato soup

This combination of chickpeas with tomatoes can be varied by using almost any other kind of canned pulses.

2 tablespoons oil
2 leeks, sliced
1 can chopped Italian tomatoes
1 can chick peas, drained
1 litre ($1\frac{3}{4}$ pints) stock *or* water + 1 stock cube
salt and pepper

Heat the oil in a large pan and add the sliced leeks, cover and let them sweat over a low heat for 10 minutes. Add the cans of tomatoes, chickpeas and the liquid and stock cube. Season with $\frac{1}{2}$ teaspoon salt and a sprinkling of pepper. This soup can be eaten as it is or puréed using a potato masher, Mouli-légumes or hand-held electric blender.

LIfe-saver soup

This Provençal soup known as *aigo bouido* is not perhaps for every day but is guaranteed to be a veritable life-saver after a heavy night on the tiles. It relies on a hefty amount of garlic and sprigs of sage, so if you think you'll often need it, grow some sage in a pot!

1 whole head of garlic
1 litre (1¾ pints, 3 mugs) water
4 sprigs of sage
2 tablespoons oil
salt

Separate the garlic into cloves, peel them and put them into a saucepan with the water, sage, oil and a generous pinch of salt. Bring to the boil and simmer the soup briskly for 15 minutes. The cloves of garlic will soften and almost melt in the mouth.

Scotch broth

This robust cross between a soup and a stew is a cheap and cheerful dish for two or three servings and because it reheats beautifully, any left-overs can be eaten the following day. To do this bring the pan to the boil, cover and leave to simmer for 15–20 minutes.

450 g (1 lb) scrag end of lamb, cut in portions
450 g (1 lb) mix of vegetables, such as carrot, onion, turnip, leek, potato all chopped or sliced
1 litre (1¾ pints, 4 mugs) stock *or* water + 1 stock cube
3 tablespoons pearl barley
salt and pepper

Trim away most of the outer fat from the lamb and put it into a large saucepan with all the vegetables. Pour over the liquid and crumble in the stock cube. Season with salt and pepper. Bring to the bowl, skim off the scum that forms on top and add the pearl barley. Cover the pan, turn the heat very low and let it simmer for 2 hours.

Fish soup

2 leeks
2 potatoes
2 carrots
1 tablespoon oil
1 clove garlic, chopped
600 ml (1 pint, 2 mugs) water
1 can Italian chopped tomatoes
salt and pepper
450 g (1 lb) fillet of firm fish such as coley, haddock, cod or hoki

Slice or chop the vegetables. Heat the oil in a saucepan, add the vegetables and garlic, cover and let them sweat over a low heat for 10 minutes. Add the water and tomatoes, season to taste with salt and pepper and bring to the boil. Cover the pan, lower the heat and simmer for 10 minutes. Cut the fish into bite-sized chunks and add to the pan. Simmer a further 5–10 minutes.

Stock

The word *stock* crops up in every cookbook and in lots of recipes. It's one of those ambiguous words that convey nothing of their meaning to the uninitiated. Basically it refers to that mythical stock-pot which in the olden days was always kept bubbling by the stove and contained all the bones and bits of left-over vegetables, the liquid from which was full of goodness and was used to give flavour to soups and stews. Mostly you won't have the time or inclination to make any but will use stock cubes or other flavourings instead. However, the water in which you've cooked vegetables can be used in its place or very occasionally you might decide you have the wherewithal to make your own. If you do, here is how to go about it.

chicken carcass or a ham bone or left-over meat bones
1 onion
1 carrot
herbs such as a bayleaf, thyme and parsley
pepper or $\frac{1}{2}$ teaspoon whole peppercorns
1 litre ($1\frac{3}{4}$ pints, 3 mugs) water

Break the carcass into small pieces. Put it with all the other ingredients into a large saucepan. Bring to the boil, lower the heat and simmer uncovered for about 1 hour. If scum forms on the top, skim it off with a spoon. When the stock is cooked, strain it into a clean bowl, using a colander. Let it cool, then refrigerate. Before using, carefully remove the hard layer of fat which will have formed on the top.

Omelettes

Omelettes, perfect single-pan meals, crop up wherever there are eggs to be broken. In Spain they call them *tortillas* and in Italy *frittatas*. They vary from plain and simple to ones filled with all sorts of delicious ingredients. A classic French omelette is always cooked in butter but this rule is not observed in places where oil is the main cooking agent. You can use which you want and even margarine if necessary.

To make a successful omelette, there are a few basic guidelines to follow:

1. The frying pan must be absolutely clean and dry, otherwise the omelette will stick.
2. Beat the eggs just sufficiently to incorporate the white with the yolk.
3. Cook the omelette in hot fat (either butter or margarine) or oil over a high heat.

Plain omelette

2 eggs
1 teaspoon cold water
salt and pepper
1 tablespoon butter, oil or margarine

Break the eggs into a bowl, add the cold water and beat them until they are mixed and slightly frothy. Add a little salt and pepper. Heat the butter, oil or margarine in a small frying pan over a medium heat. When it begins to foam and splutter, raise the heat and pour in the egg mixture. Let it settle and begin to set, then lift the edge all round with a spatula, so that the uncooked mixture runs underneath. Continue to do this until the omelette is set but still glistening. Using a spatula, fold the omelette in half and slide it on to your plate.

Omelette fillings

There are all sorts of fillings and toppings for omelettes. You can add filling just before you fold the omelette over, or, if there is a lot of it, simply pile it on top of the omelette and put the whole thing under the grill to brown a little. Below are some suggestions. Choose just one or combine two or three, whatever takes your fancy.

- *Aubergine* – sliced and fried in oil.
- *Bacon* – a chopped rasher or two, fried or grilled.
- *Bread* – cubed and gently fried.
- *Cheese* – 1 or 2 tablespoons grated Cheddar or similar hard cheese, cottage, curd or goat's.
- *Courgette* – sliced and lightly fried.
- *Fish* – canned tuna, sardines or pilchards.
- *Herbs* – ½ teaspoonful of dried mixed herbs, or a single herb like thyme, parsley or oregano.
- *Meat* – almost any kind of cooked meat, finely sliced, especially ham or chicken or Continental sausages like salami or Spanish *chorizo*, which is mildly flavoured with garlic and paprika.
- *Mushrooms* – finely sliced and fried in a little oil.
- *Onion* – chopped and fried in a little oil until lightly browned.
- *Peas* – canned, one or two tablespoons heated through.
- *Pimientos* – canned, well drained and cut in slices.
- *Potato* – a chopped cooked potato, or a raw potato cut into small pieces and fried in a little oil until soft, 5–10 minutes.
- *Pulses* – half a mugful of any canned dried beans such as chick-peas, flageolet, haricot or butter beans, heated through .
- *Tomato* – sliced and lightly fried.
- *Sweetcorn* – canned, one or two tablespoons, heated through.
- *Sweet pepper* – sliced and lightly fried.
- *Vegetables* – cooked and chopped, such as spinach, carrots, cauli-flower, broccoli.

Omelettes can also be filled with sweet things. Use almost any kind of dried fruit or fresh fruit, sliced and fried in a little oil or butter, such as apples, pears, bananas, pineapple or strawberries. Or perhaps, least complicated of all, a spoonful or two of your favourite jam or honey.

Pipérade

This is a dish from the Basque country and is a cross between an omelette and scrambled eggs.

2 tablespoons oil
1 onion, chopped
$1/2$ sweet pepper, thinly sliced
2 tomatoes, chopped
salt and pepper
$1/4$ teaspoon dried oregano
2 eggs

Heat the oil in a frying pan and add the chopped onion, let it fry gently until soft, about 10 minutes. Add the sliced pepper and cook a further 5 minutes, stirring from time to time. Add the chopped tomatoes, season with salt and pepper and sprinkle over the oregano. Mix well, lower the heat and cover with either a lid or a piece of foil. Meanwhile break the eggs into a bowl and beat them until frothy. Pour the egg mixture over the vegetables in the pan and stir gently until they set but are still moist and glistening.

Pizzas

The pizza is another successful single-pan meal, which has become almost as much of a national dish as fish and chips. Pizzas are sold everywhere from take-aways to supermarkets and the smallest corner shop, varying in quality from sublime to abysmal. The perfect student food, except for the price. You can save a lot by making your own.

The traditional Italian base is made of bread dough. Ready-made bases are widely available, especially in supermarkets, but although they are intensely labour-saving, they too are not exactly cheap. A better buy are packets of ready-mix bases which need only the addition of water and a short kneading period. All that remains is to add a topping to the base, stick the whole thing in a hot oven for 20–30 minutes and presto!

The cheapest option, though the most time-consuming, is to make your own pizza base using the basic ingredients of flour, salt, sugar, fast-action yeast, oil and water. Not perhaps to be undertaken when you come home tired and hungry on a weekday evening because the dough must be kneaded for 10 minutes and then set aside for at least 30 minutes, but quite practical at weekends.

If you're not too worried about tradition and are really pressed for time but still want to make your own base, you could make it by using a scone or potato mixture, neither of which uses yeast and so requires no kneading or rising time. Pizzas made with either of these bases can be cooked in a frying pan or in the oven.

Or, for an almost instant snack, you could cheat completely and use toasted muffins or crumpets on which to build your topping, or Italian or French bread split lengthwise or even Naan or pitta bread sliced in half. You could even use toast. Once assembled, simply put under a hot grill for a few minutes.

Skip to page 54 if you just want ideas for pizza toppings.

Traditional pizza base

150 g (6 oz, 1 mug) flour
½ teaspoon salt
½ teaspoon sugar
½ teaspoon fast-action yeast
½ tablespoon oil
2 tablespoons boiling water mixed with 4 tablespoons cold water

Put flour, salt, sugar and yeast into a bowl and mix well. Make a hollow in the centre and add the oil and water. Mix with a knife to form a stiff dough. To prevent the dough from sticking, sprinkle your hands and a board with flour. Form the dough into a ball. Knead it on the board by flattening it with the heel of your hand, gathering it into a ball and flattening again. Repeat this process for about 10 minutes, turning the dough to make you sure you knead every part, until it becomes pliable and elastic and no longer sticky. Sprinkle the board and a rolling pin (or bottle) with more flour and roll the dough out into a circle of about 25 cm (10 ins) diameter. Set aside for at least 30 minutes to rise.

Add your chosen topping (see page 54) and cook on a baking sheet, smeared with a little oil, in an oven heated to Gas 7/425°F/220°C for 25 minutes.

Scone pizza base

150 g (6 oz, 1 mug) self-raising flour or
use plain flour and add 1 teaspoon baking powder
pinch salt
1 tablespoon oil
2–3 tablespoons water

Put the flour and salt into a bowl, make a hollow in the centre, add the oil and 1 tablespoon of the water. Mix with a knife, adding just sufficient water to make a firm and spongy dough. Put some flour on your hands and on a board and form the dough into a ball. Roll it out into a circle of about 20 cm (8 in).

Add your chosen topping (see page 54) and cook on a baking sheet, smeared with a little oil, in an oven heated to Gas 7/425°F/220°C for 25 minutes.

Alternatively, heat 1 tablespoon of oil in a frying pan, add the dough and fry over a medium heat for about 5 minutes until the underside is golden. Turn it over, add your chosen topping (see page 54), cover the pan, lower the heat and cook until the base is golden and the topping heated through, 15–20 minutes. You can then put it under a hot grill for 2–3 minutes to brown the top if you wish.

Potato pizza base

$^1/_2$ mug cold mashed potato
salt and pepper
1 tablespoon oil
3 tablespoons plain flour
$^1/_4$ teaspoon baking powder
1–2 tablespoons water or milk

Using a knife, mix the mashed potato with a pinch of salt, some pepper and the oil. Mix in the flour and baking powder and sufficient water or milk to form a dough. Put some flour on your hands and on a board and form the ball into a dough. Roll it out on the board into a circle about 20 cm (8 in) in diameter.

Add your chosen topping (see page 54) and cook on a baking sheet, smeared with a little oil, in an oven heated to Gas 7/425°F/220°C for 25 minutes.

Alternatively, heat a tablespoon of oil in a frying pan, add the base and your chosen topping (see page 54) , cover and fry over a medium heat for about 20–25 minutes. Check half-way through to make sure the base is not getting too brown; if necessary lower the heat. Brown under a hot grill for 2–3 minutes if you wish.

Basic pizza topping

Almost all pizzas have sliced or chopped tomatoes as a base. These can be fresh or canned. If using the latter make sure they are well drained. Bottled Italian tomato and pizza toppings are widely available and make great standbys but are rather expensive.

$\frac{1}{2}$ tablespoon oil
100–150 g (4–6 oz) fresh or canned tomatoes, finely sliced or
   chopped *or*
2–3 tablespoons bottled Italian tomato or pizza sauce
1 clove garlic, finely chopped or crushed, optional
salt and pepper
$\frac{1}{2}$ teaspoon dried oregano or marjoram

Sprinkle the base with the oil and cover it completely with a layer of tomatoes. Sprinkle over the garlic and oregano or marjoram and season with salt and pepper. Add further ingredients according to what you fancy, ringing the changes to suit yourself. Sprinkle with a little more oil before cooking.

Further pizza ingredients

- *Cheese* – sliced or grated. Choose from a hard English variety like Cheddar, Leicester or Red Cheshire or go for soft curd cheeses made from cow's, goat's or ewe's milk. Or for special days be extravagant and treat yourself to Mozzarella.
- *Fish* – canned, such as anchovy fillets, tuna, mussels, sardines or pilchards.
- *Meat* – almost any kind of cooked meat, finely sliced, especially ham or Italian sausage like salami or smoked sausage cut in thin rings.
- *Olives* – black or green.
- *Vegetables* – canned – such as sweetcorn or pimientos; or for a treat, artichoke hearts cut in half or asparagus pieces; fresh – such as raw mushrooms or sweet peppers, finely sliced; or onion,

aubergine or courgettes, sliced and fried in a little oil before using. Look out for jars of Italian vegetables preserved in oil sold in some supermarkets. These include sun-dried tomatoes, artichoke hearts, mushrooms and peppers.

Pulses mean beans

It seems that all the world has known the value of pulses or dried beans for centuries but, perhaps because of their nickname *poor man's meat*, we in Britain have, until recently, treated them as a joke. However, it's worth forgetting any prejudices you may hold about pulses belonging to the lunatic fringe of faddy eaters because they are very good news indeed, being both cheap and nutritious. The secret of getting the most of their proteins is to combine them with things like grains, nuts and seeds or any kind of dairy produce or eggs. So you can now feel virtuous every time you heat up a can of baked beans and have them on toast, or eat a piece of bread with peanut butter or *hummus*, which is made from chickpeas, garlic and sesame seeds. These are perfect instant snacks.

You can buy pulses either dried or ready-cooked in cans. The former are cheaper but their preparation is more time-consuming, especially those that need to be soaked, and when you first read instructions you can be forgiven for wanting to grab the nearest can opener. So begin by doing just that, try a few canned varieties first and if you then have the time and inclination then go for cooking your own.

Canned beans or indeed any left-over pulses can be eaten cold as a salad, in which case season them while still warm with a squeeze of lemon juice, add a sprinkling of oil and either a raw onion, finely cut in rings, or a chopped clove of garlic. You can turn them into a satisfying cold meal by adding things like canned tuna, sardines, mussels or pilchards.

Below are some recipes for some easy single-pan meals, and on page 61 you will find instructions on how to soak and cook different kinds of dried beans.

Dhal

This spicy Indian dish uses split red lentils which need no preliminary soaking. It can be quite simple as in the recipe below or you can jazz it up by including a sliced red or green pepper and a couple of tomatoes. Eat the dhal with Naan bread, which, like root ginger, is sold in supermarkets and ethnic shops. Buy the ginger in a smallish piece. Cut a fine sliver from it and store the remaining ginger in a cool place; the cut side heals itself.

1 mug of red split lentils
$2\frac{1}{4}$ mugs water
1 bayleaf
1 small onion, chopped
1 clove garlic, crushed
a sliver of ginger, finely chopped
$\frac{1}{2}$ teaspoon ground cumin

Put all the ingredients into a saucepan over a high heat. Bring to the boil, lower heat and simmer for about 30 minutes until the lentils are soft and have absorbed the water.

Haricot beans with bacon and onion

You could just as easily use almost any other kind of pulse in this way.

1 tablespoon oil
2 rashers of bacon, chopped
1 onion, chopped
1 can or 1 mug cooked haricot beans
salt and pepper
toast

Heat the oil in a saucepan or wok and fry the chopped bacon and onion until soft and golden, 5–10 minutes. Stir in the haricot beans and season with salt and pepper. Heat until piping hot and eat on the toast.

Vary the above recipe by substituting a couple of chopped tomatoes for the bacon and stirring in a small can of tuna fish.

Chickpeas with potato and onion

1 tablespoon oil
1 onion, chopped
1 potato, peeled and cut in small pieces
1/2 teaspoon turmeric
1 can or 1 mugful cooked chickpeas
salt
1/2 teaspoon sugar
toast

Heat the oil in a saucepan or wok and add the chopped onion and potato cut in small pieces. Cook gently, stirring from time to time, until the onions and potatoes are soft, 10–15 minutes. Stir in the turmeric and chickpeas and season with salt and the sugar. Heat until piping hot. Eat on toast.

Pulses with vegetables

All kinds of canned or cooked pulses can be mixed with all kinds of vegetables and it is not hard to devise your own dishes. The basic method remains the same. You can use whatever vegetables you like, choosing from leeks, courgettes, tomatoes, mushrooms, sweet peppers, aubergines, turnips, runner beans, mangetout, Chinese leaves or sugar-snap peas – whatever is in season, in fact. The secret is to slice or chop them small. If you have some herbs or spices, add a dash of one or two, being careful not to overdo it or you'll negate the flavours.

1 tablespoon oil
sliver of root ginger, chopped small
1 onion, chopped
1 clove garlic, chopped

chosen vegetables, chopped, see above
1 mug canned or cooked pulses
1 tablespoon soy sauce
salt and pepper

Heat the oil in a saucepan or wok and add the chopped ginger, onion and garlic. Fry them for a minute or two, then stir in the chopped vegetables. Stir-fry them over a medium heat for a few minutes, then add the pulses, soy sauce and a seasoning of salt and pepper and herbs or spices if using. Cover the pan and set over a low heat for 5–10 minutes until everything is piping hot.

Rice and beans

All over south America there are recipes for rice and beans from the Cuban *Moors and Christians,* made with black beans and white rice, to Jamaica's *Rice and peas,* traditionally made using pigeon peas or dried red beans. They make wonderfully filling and tasty single-pan meals and are full of nutrition. If you're especially hungry, top them with a fried egg. They are almost all made in much the same way, the only difference being in the flavouring. Some use hot chillies, others paprika or cumin or herbs like bayleaves and thyme.

The following basic recipe uses canned red kidney beans but it can be varied by using almost any other kind of pulse and even by substituting the rice with another kind of grain like bulgar wheat, buckwheat, millet or couscous. Cooking times may vary, so see page 87 for more details on these grains.

1 tablespoon oil
1 onion, chopped
1 clove garlic, chopped, optional
$\frac{1}{2}$ green pepper, deseeded and chopped
1 tomato, chopped
1 can or 1 mug of cooked red kidney beans
$\frac{1}{2}$ mug white rice

1 mug water
salt and pepper

Heat the oil in a saucepan and fry the chopped onion, garlic and pepper for a few moments over a medium heat. Add the chopped tomato and cook for a minute or two longer before stirring in the beans, rice and water. Season with the salt and pepper, bring to the boil and cover. Lower the heat to the lowest possible setting and simmer for 20 minutes. Remove the pan from the heat and set aside for 10 minutes before lifting the lid.

Kicheri

This recipe is based on one that appears in my other student book *Vegetarian Student*. It is the dish that our popular *kedgeree* derives from and is made from mung beans, which don't need any preliminary soaking, mixed with brown rice and an assortment of vegetables.

4 tablespoons mung beans
4 tablespoons brown rice
1 onion or 1 clove garlic, chopped
sliver root ginger, finely chopped
1 potato, unpeeled and chopped
2 carrots, sliced
1 tablespoon oil
1 mug water
1 tablespoon soy sauce
squeeze lemon juice
salt and pepper
1 tomato, chopped

Put all the ingredients except the lemon juice, salt and tomato into a large saucepan. Bring to the boil, stir well, cover the pot and simmer for 45 minutes. Turn off the heat and leave to stand for 10 minutes without lifting the cover. Add the lemon juice and a seasoning of salt and pepper and stir in the chopped tomato.

How to soak and cook dried beans

Beans swell during cooking to two to three times their original size. 1 mugful of uncooked beans will be enough for three or four helpings. Some pulses don't need soaking. These are lentils, both whole and split, split peas, mung beans and black-eyed beans.

Pulses that need soaking include aduki beans, black beans, butter beans, cannellini beans, chickpeas, haricot beans, red kidney beans and soya beans. There are two methods of soaking.

1. Put them in a large saucepan, cover with water, bring to the boil and simmer for five minutes. Remove from the heat and set aside for 1 hour. Drain.
2. Soak them overnight or for several hours in cold water. Drain. (This method is most suitable for the kinds of beans which take longest to cook e.g. chickpeas and soya beans which benefit from being soaked for up to 24 hours.)

To cook pulses

Use a large saucepan, add the pulses and cover them generously with fresh water. Add no salt as this inhibits the softening process. Bring to the boil and boil hard for 10 minutes – this will kill any toxics in the beans – then lower the heat, cover and simmer for the appropriate time. Test after this and if they are not quite soft, simmer a little longer.

The table overleaf gives an indication of how long you should cook various pulses.

Cooking times for pulses in minutes

Split red lentils	20–30
Aduki beans Mung beans Split peas	30–45
Black-eyed beans Whole lentils	45–60
Black beans Cannellini beans Red kidney beans	60
Butter beans Chickpeas Haricot beans	90
Soya beans	Up to 180

Parcels

This is single-pan cooking at its best. In fact all you need is a baking sheet and some foil in which the food is parcelled to go into the oven for 20–30 minutes, from where it emerges perfectly cooked. Ideal for days when you're cooking jacket potatoes or there's more than just yourself to feed. Serve the cooked parcels just as they are so that the unwrapping is done at the table, thus releasing all the succulent flavours.

The method

Cut an oblong of foil amply large enough to wrap your filling, sprinkle it with a little oil, lay the food in the centre. Make a parcel by bringing the two longest edges together and pleating them together twice. Twist each end of the parcel to secure.

Heat the oven to Gas 5/375°F/190°C, put the parcel(s) on a baking sheet and put into the oven for the times stated below.

Parcel fillings

- *Fish* – spread a whole fish like mackerel or herring with mustard, season with salt and pepper and lemon juice. Fish steaks or fillets (coley and plaice are two of the cheapest) can be flavoured by adding a chopped tomato or mushroom and seasoned with lemon juice, salt and pepper. Cook for 20 minutes.
- *Meat* – this could be chicken or turkey breasts or joints, rabbit joints, lamb or pork chops or escalopes or gammon steaks. Sprinkle the meat with a little lemon juice or soya sauce and season it with salt and pepper, add flavour by either spreading with a little mustard, honey or pesto sauce or sprinkling over chopped dried herbs such as thyme or rosemary. For a change put slices of apple on top of pork or gammon. Cook for 25 minutes or, in the case of pork, for 35.
- *Vegetables* – all kinds of vegetables can be baked in parcels. Slice

them before putting them on the oiled foil and adding salt and pepper. Carrots and courgettes take about 40 minutes, onions and parsnips 45–50.

Garlic and herb breads

These are widely available in supermarkets but they are more expensive than making your own. The basic method remains the same. You need a piece of foil large enough to enclose the loaf. You can ring the changes by adding some pieces of sun-dried tomatoes or by using pesto instead of the butter or oil.

1 long French or Italian loaf
25–50g (1–2 oz) butter or 2–4 tablespoons oil
1 clove garlic, chopped or sprinkling mixed herbs

Slice the bread but don't cut it right through in order that the loaf still holds together. Either spread the loaf all over with butter or sprinkle it with the oil. Sprinkle the garlic or herbs on top. Wrap in foil and bake in a hot oven Gas 7/425°F/220°C for 10 minutes.

Fruit

Fruit can also be cooked in parcels. The recipe is for bananas or apples but you could equally use almost any kind of fruit. Especially delicious are peaches and pears.

1 banana or apple sliced
squeeze of lemon juice
pinch of nutmeg or cinnamon
1 tablespoon sugar, honey, marmalade or jam

Lay the sliced fruit on a sheet of foil, add the lemon juice, nutmeg or cinnamon and the sugar, honey, marmalade or jam. Seal the parcel and bake for 15 minutes at Gas 5/375°F/190°C.

Fish

If you limit yourself to buying fish from a frozen food counter, you can be forgiven for thinking the choice is sparse and expensive although there seems to be an endless supply of those old favourites, cod and haddock coated in batter or breadcrumbs.

Fortunately, in spite of the nation's conservative attitude to fish, which dictates that only a few species are truly acceptable, there are a host of other kinds which are relatively cheap. So be prepared to be adventurous. You won't find many of them among the frozen fish so you will need to discover a fishmonger's or go to the fish counter in your local supermarket (see page 11 for notes on how to choose a fresh fish).

Most fish is seasonal, so the secret of buying it is to see what's on the slab and choose accordingly. The cheaper kinds include: cat- and dogfish (sold under aliases like rock fish, rock salmon, rock turbot, huss, flake or rig), coley, conger eel, dab, flounder or fluke, garfish, grey mullet, herring, hoki, horse mackerel, mackerel, mussels, plaice, pollack, redfish, sardines, snappers, sprats, squid, whiting and witch.

Grilled fish

You can grill whole fish or fillets or steaks. If grilling whole fish make two diagonal slits in each side with a sharp knife and, if you like garlic or ginger, insert slivers into them. (Or make kebabs by putting small pieces of fish on a skewer, alternated with quarters of tomatoes, green peppers and onion rings.)

1 whole fish or fish steak or fillet
1 tablespoon oil
$1/2$ teaspoon dried herbs
salt and pepper
squeeze of lemon juice

Heat the grill until it is very hot. Pour half the oil into the grill pan and sprinkle in the herbs and put under the grill for a minute or two to heat. When it is sizzling, add the fish, sprinkle with remaining oil, season with salt and pepper and a squeeze of lemon juice. Whole fish, fillets and kebabs need to be turned over half-way through the cooking time, but steaks can be cooked without turning.

Fish is cooked when the flesh is opaque: test with a skewer.

Grilling times

Fillets 3–4 minutes on cut side, two minutes on skin side.
Whole fish 4–7 minutes on each side.
Steaks 8–15 minutes depending on thickness (cook without turning).
Kebabs about 12 minutes (turning frequently).

Poached fish

This method is especially suitable for smoked fish such as kippers or haddock. Simply lay the fish in a saucepan and just cover it with water, or milk for haddock, bring just to boiling point. Cover and let it barely simmer over the lowest possible heat for 5–10 minutes until the flesh is opaque.

Kippers cooked in a jug

Try this old-fashioned way of poaching kippers. Put a kipper in a jug, fill up with boiling water. Leave for 5 minutes. Remove from the jug and eat topped with a lump of butter.

Fried fish

Deep frying, the method used for standard fish and chips, is an expensive exercise. Shallow frying, which uses very little oil or fat, is a cheaper alternative. It is suitable for small whole fish, cutlets, steaks and fillets. Rolling the fish in flour prevents it from sticking to the pan, but don't worry if you have no flour, just make sure the oil is really hot before you begin frying. (If you want to eat chips with your fish, the best bet is to buy frozen oven chips which are simply heated in the oven.)

1 tablespoon flour
salt and pepper
1 whole fish, steak or fillet
2 tablespoons oil
squeeze of lemon juice

Put the flour on a plate, add a little salt and pepper and roll the fish in it so that it is evenly coated all over. Heat the oil in a frying pan and, when it is hot, add the fish and fry over a medium heat until golden. Turn it over, lower the heat and fry gently for a further 5–6 minutes until the flesh is firm and opaque. Squeeze over the lemon juice.

Baked fish

The easiest way of baking individual portions of fish is in foil parcels, see page 68.

Steamed fish

Forget about notions that steamed fish is invalid food: it is delicious and very easy to prepare and if you are cooking a vegetable accompaniment, the whole process can be done using the same saucepan. You can steam the fish on a buttered plate or use one of those collapsible vegetable steamers, or if you have a wok buy a Chinese wooden steamer to stand over it. Below is a basic recipe but you can add interest by scoring the fish with a sharp knife and inserting thin slivers of garlic or root ginger and sprinkling it with soy sauce and perhaps a few chopped mushrooms or a sliced green pepper or simply spread it with a tablespoon of pesto sauce.

1 whole fish or a fish steak or fillet
salt and pepper
squeeze of lemon juice
$1/4$ teaspoon dried herbs, or thyme or parsley

Lay the fish on a buttered plate or in the steamer basket. Season it with salt and pepper and sprinkle with the herbs. Put on a lid and stand it over simmering water until it is cooked. It will turn opaque. Test after 5–7 minutes, but it may take longer depending on the thickness of the fish.

Stir-fry

This is where your wok comes into its own. Invented by the Chinese, it's the perfect receptacle for cooking one-pan meals and stir-frying. This method is both quick and highly nutritious, especially for vegetables which are cooked for the minimum of time, thus retaining their crispness and freshness. You can stir-fry a single vegetable or a combination of meat, fish and vegetables, perhaps with added pulses, eggs or cheese.

The secret of stir-frying is to prepare all the ingredients before you begin, cutting everything into small, even pieces. Once everything is ready, the wok is heated over a medium flame with a little oil and the stir-frying can begin. The Chinese often begin by frying a small sliver of root ginger, finely chopped, which gives a sweet, peppery flavour to the dish, followed by garlic, onion or leek. Stir-frying means what it says. Simply keep stirring and frying using a wooden spatula.

Stir-fried vegetables

Almost all vegetables can be stir-fried. Hard vegetables obviously take longer than soft ones, but you simply cook the hard ones first and add the softer ones after a few minutes. With a bit of practice you will soon get the hang of it.

2 tablespoons oil
sliver of root ginger, finely chopped
1 onion, leek or clove of garlic, chopped
one or several vegetables, cut into small even-sized pieces
a little water
salt and pepper
soy sauce

Heat the oil in the wok over a medium heat and fry the chopped ginger and onion, leek or garlic for 2–3 minutes. Add the harder vegetables, like carrots or sweet peppers, and stir-fry for 3 minutes. Add softer vegetables like mushrooms or tomatoes and continue to stir-fry until all the vegetables are hot but still crisp. Add the water, put on the lid and simmer over a low heat for 3–4 minutes. Add salt and pepper to taste and a sprinkling of soy sauce.

Variations

To make the above into more of a meal, try adding one of the following variations.

- *Beansprouts* – these are sold in many supermarkets and greengrocers (or grow your own, see page 138). Add a handful or two at the end of the cooking time and stir-fry until hot through.
- *Nuts and seeds* – add about 1 tablespoon of any chopped nuts such as almonds, hazelnuts, walnuts or mixed nuts or 1 teaspoon sesame, sunflower or pumpkin seeds.
- *Pulses* – stir in $\frac{1}{2}$ mugful of any canned or cooked pulses, once hot through, sprinkle in 2–3 tablespoons grated cheese or small pieces of curd cheese.
- *Rice or other grains* – stir in $\frac{1}{2}$ mugful any cooked grains, break in an egg, stir well for 2–3 minutes until hot through.

Stir-fried chicken or turkey

Chicken or turkey breasts take only a few minutes cooked in this way and need nothing to accompany them except some good crusty bread and perhaps a green salad. If you haven't any parsley, never mind, but it does add an attractive quality to the finished dish as well as taking away the strong effects of garlic on the breath!

1 chicken or turkey breast
lemon juice
pepper
1 tablespoon oil
soy sauce
sliver root ginger, finely chopped

1 clove garlic, finely chopped
1 tablespoon chopped fresh parsley

Remove any skin from the chicken or turkey breast. Slice the meat into thin strips about 5 mm ($^1/_4$ in) wide. Put them in a shallow dish and sprinkle over some lemon juice (don't use a metal dish because the acidic lemon will cause a toxic reaction). Season with pepper. Set aside for 30 minutes or so before cooking. This will tenderize the meat and give it flavour.

To cook: Heat the oil in a wok or frying pan, add the sliced chicken and stir-fry it over a high heat for a minute or two. Lower the heat to medium and continue to stir for 3–4 minutes, the chicken will feel springy when pressed and be turning golden. Sprinkle with a few drops of soy sauce, add the chopped ginger, garlic and parsley. Stir for 1 minute and serve.

Stir-fried chicken livers with salad

This dish which has now become something of a restaurant cliché started life as an economical meal for a French peasant. Pig's liver was the most likely ingredient but chicken or turkey livers are to be preferred. They are sold frozen in many supermarkets and must be allowed to thoroughly defrost before cooking. Packs usually contain 225 g (8 oz) which may be too much for one meal, depending on appetites. However, any left over can be mashed with a little butter or margarine and used to make a sandwich spread.

sufficient lettuce or spinach leaves for a salad
1 tablespoon plain flour
salt and pepper
225 g (8 oz) chicken or turkey livers
2 tablespoons oil
1 clove garlic, chopped
$^1/_2$ teaspoon dried mixed herbs or dried thyme
$^1/_2$ tablespoon soy sauce

Wash the lettuce or spinach and dry it either between pieces of kitchen paper or by shaking in a colander. Put on a plate.

Put the flour with a little salt and pepper into a plastic bag. Cut the livers into thin strips and put them into the bag. Shake it so that the meat is coated with the flour. Heat the oil in a wok or frying pan and when it is hot, stir-fry the livers over a medium heat, until they are brown all over. Add the garlic and herbs and stir-fry for 2 or 3 minutes longer before sprinkling with the soy sauce. Pile on to the salad and serve.

Stir-fried mince and courgette

This dish can be eaten between pieces of pitta bread, with pasta or rice or with potatoes. Instead of the courgette, you could use an aubergine, mushrooms, tomatoes, mangetout, celery, broccoli or what you will.

2 tablespoons oil
1 courgette, finely sliced
$1/4$ pint water plus $1/2$ stock cube
100 g (4 oz) mince
sliver root ginger, finely sliced
soy sauce
salt and pepper

Heat half the oil in a wok or frying pan and add the finely sliced courgette. Stir-fry over a medium heat for 2–3 minutes, add the water, crumble in the $1/2$ stock cube, put on the lid and simmer gently for 6–7 minutes. Put the courgette and liquid on a plate and set aside. Heat the remaining oil and when it sizzles, stir in the mince and ginger. Stir-fry over a high heat for 3–4 minutes until brown all over. Return the courgettes and their cooking liquid to the pan, add a sprinkling of soy sauce and season to taste with salt and pepper.

Stir-fried fish

You need firm fish for this dish, which is particularly good eaten with rice. Choose cod, haddock or a cheaper kind such as rock salmon (see page 65 for its aliases), or hoki, coley or conger eel. If you buy coley, don't be put off by its greyness: it turns pristine white when cooked.

150–225 g (6–8 oz) firm white fish, either steak or fillet
1 tablespoon oil
sliver root ginger, finely chopped
1 small onion, finely sliced
soy sauce
2 tablespoons water and $\frac{1}{2}$ a stock cube

Cut the fish into bite-sized chunks and remove any bones and skin. Heat the oil in a wok or frying pan and fry the ginger and onion over a medium heat for 1–2 minutes. Add the chunks of fish, one piece at a time and let them fry without turning for a minute or two. Turn them over and continue to fry each side, until they are opaque all over. Avoid too much heavy stirring or the fish will break up. Add the soy sauce and water and crumble in the stock cube. As soon as the liquid boils, lower the heat, cover and allow to barely simmer for 3–4 minutes before serving.

Grilled meats and hamburgers

Grilled meat

Grilling is one of the quickest methods of providing a meal in a hurry. It's not a cheap option as the cuts of meat you can use need to be lean and tender. If the meat has been frozen make sure it has completely thawed before you cook it and if it's been in the fridge, take it out at least 30 minutes ahead of time, because meat that is chilled will be tough. (You can speed up the thawing process a bit by putting it under running cold water, never hot as this just encourages bacteria.) If you're being completely extravagant and going for steak the cuts to go for are rump, sirloin or porterhouse; fillet is the tenderest but very costly.

This sort of meal is delicious eaten with something quite simple like a good hunk of bread and a plain salad. Or if you feel you must have something more substantial, bake a jacket or sweet potato or heat up a packet of oven chips.

You can grill meat just as it is but if there's time, it improves the flavour and texture if you marinate it first for at least 30 minutes.

lemon juice
pepper
a sprig of fresh rosemary or thyme or $1/2$ teaspoon
    mixed dried herbs
1 chicken joint or 1 chop or escalope of pork
    or lamb chop or a steak

If you are going to marinate the meat, put it in a china or glass dish (not metal, which acts adversely with lemon juice), sprinkle with a little lemon juice, season with pepper – no salt, which simply makes the juices run and toughens the meat – and put the herbs on top. Cover and leave for 30 minutes.

To cook: Heat the grill and pan until it is very hot, about 5 minutes. Add the meat which will immediately be seared when it comes into contact with the heat. Grill it for 3–4 minutes before turning over and lowering the heat. Continue grilling, allowing the specified times in total.

Chicken joint Test it is done by inserting a skewer in the thickest part, the juice should run clear. If pink, continue grilling for a little longer.	15–20 minutes – turning every 5 minutes
Lamb chop or escalope	8–12 minutes – turning once
Pork chop or escalope Test as for chicken	15–20 minutes – turning once
Steak Allow 150 g (6 oz) per head	Rare – 3 minutes each side Medium – 5 minutes each side Well done – 8–10 minutes each side

Fried meat

These cuts of meat can also be fried though it is not such a satisfactory method. Make sure the pan is very hot before you begin to cook and follow cooking guidelines above, frying the meat in a tablespoon or two of oil.

Hamburgers

These are simple to make and much cheaper than bought varieties. You can vary the mixture by adding a tablespoon of grated cheese or a little mustard. The finished hamburgers can be topped with grated blue-vein or plain cheese, or sweetcorn and chopped apple or a tablespoon or two of chilli sauce, pickles or relish. Eat them as they are or sandwiched between soft rolls. As an alternative to beef, use minced chicken, lamb, pork or even venison.

100 g (4 oz) mince
1 teaspoon finely chopped onion
salt and pepper
1 tablespoon oil

Mix the mince with the onion, salt and pepper. With wet hands, shape the mixture into two balls, then flatten into cakes about 1 cm (½ in) thick. Heat the oil in a frying pan and when it is very hot, add the cakes, cook them over a high heat, allowing about 5 minutes on each side. (The fierce heat will prevent the hamburgers breaking up as they are cooking.)

Potato burgers

Follow the above recipe but use equal quantities of mince and mashed potatoes.

Two-pan meals

Pasta

The Italians – or was it the Chinese? – knew what they were about when they invented pasta and the huge varieties of sauces with which it is eaten. Most pasta dishes are quick to prepare and provide highly satisfying two-pan meals. Pasta comes in dozens of different shapes and sizes, each one, it seems, designed to match the sauce that accompanies it. All a bit confusing for the novice cook. It's simplest if you begin with one long shape like *spaghetti* or *tagliatelle* and one spiral or butterfly shape like *farfalle* or *fusilli*, then go on to experiment with others. Above all, don't feel intimidated when you do come across recipes which specify particular shapes, as they'll mostly work with other kinds.

You can buy pasta either dried or fresh. The former is widely available and keeps well and is the kind the Italians use except for special occasions. Fresh pasta is more expensive but only needs to be cooked for a few minutes and it does have a particularly good flavour. Pasta is made from whole durum wheat and some kinds are enriched with eggs. Also available is wholemeal pasta, which has a nuttier flavour but tends to be a little heavy.

Look out too for Chinese egg noodles which take only a few minutes to cook and go well with stir-fried dishes.

As well as simple pastas, you can buy stuffed pasta dumplings in the form of *tortellini* or *ravioli*. *Tortellini*, modelled, so it is said, on Venus's navel, have a variety of fillings including chicken, pork, Italian sausage, cheese and nutmeg. *Ravioli* is usually filled with spinach and ricotta cheese and sometimes with meat. These pasta dumplings are often sold in supermarkets and make a quick and satisfying meal, heated and served with either grated cheese or a tomato sauce. Instructions are on packets.

Any left-over pasta can be used as a salad base or reheated by immersing in boiling water for a minute or two, then thoroughly drained.

To cook pasta

Allow 75–100 g (3–4 oz) per person (if you've no scales you'll have to guesstimate the weight).

1. Use your largest saucepan.
2. Half fill it with water and bring it to a racing boil. Add ½ teaspoon salt and 1 teaspoon oil. The oil will stop the water boiling over.
3. Add the pasta gradually, letting long shapes curl themselves into the water.
4. Keep the water boiling briskly and stir to make sure the pasta is not sticking to the base.
5. Follow cooking times on the packet or try this unconventional method: boil hard for two minutes, remove from the heat, cover the pan and leave for 10 minutes.
6. Test pasta is cooked by biting a bit. It should be *al dente*, that is, soft but still chewy. (You can throw a piece at the wall: if it sticks it is ready, but beware, it doesn't do much for the paintwork!)
7. Drain the pasta well through a colander or sieve. Return to the pan, stir in a tablespoon or two of oil or butter and season well with black pepper; if this is freshly ground through a peppermill, so much the better.
8. Instead of the oil or butter use pesto sauce, which is sold in many supermarkets as well as smaller shops. It is strongly flavoured with basil which has a pungent, peppery taste.

No-cook pasta sauces

You can of course buy ready-prepared pasta sauces and these are fine though rather expensive. For a treat, it's worth looking out for the jars of Italian *antipastos*, which include ingredients like mixed peppers, artichokes, mushrooms and sun-dried tomatoes. Although designed to be eaten as starters, they heat beautifully and provide instant pasta toppings.

If you've time to spare, it is of course cheaper to make your own sauces. Not all require cooking, which means that in a matter of minutes you can have a meal in front of you. The simplest of all is to turn the cooked pasta (which you've already dosed with oil or butter and black pepper) on to a plate and liberally sprinkle it with grated cheese. Make it more of a meal by breaking an egg into the pasta and mixing quickly to coat the pasta and cook the egg.

The Italians use herbs in many of their sauces such as parsley, oregano, rosemary and basil. Each adds its own special flavour to the dish but because they're not cheap to buy, I haven't included them in the following recipes. However, if you have some on hand, a sprinkling of one or the other, either fresh or dried, will make all the difference.

Curd cheese sauce

2 tablespoons ricotta or other curd cheese
1 tablespoon pesto sauce

Mix the curd cheese with the pesto sauce. Pile on to the pasta which has already been mixed with oil or butter and seasoned with salt and pepper.

Quick-cook pasta sauces

Thunder and lightning – tuoni e lampo

1 tablespoon oil
1 clove garlic, chopped
$\frac{1}{2}$ can chickpeas
2–3 tablespoons grated cheese

Heat the oil in a saucepan, add the garlic and cook gently for a minute or two. Stir in the chickpeas and heat through until piping hot. Pile on to the pasta which has already been mixed with oil or butter and seasoned with salt and pepper and sprinkle over the grated cheese.

This sauce can of course be made with almost any other kind of dried beans, such as flageolet, butter, haricot, cannellini etc.

Bacon and onion sauce

1 tablespoon oil
2–3 rashers bacon, chopped
1 onion, chopped
2–3 tablespoons grated cheese

Heat the oil in a saucepan, add the chopped rashers of bacon and when their fat runs out, add the chopped onion. Let them cook together for 5–10 minutes over a low heat. Pile on to the pasta which has already been mixed with oil or butter and seasoned with salt and pepper. Top with the grated cheese.

Vary the above recipe by adding two or three chopped mushrooms. Or instead of bacon use a chopped slice or two of ham, salami or other Continental sausage.

Oil and garlic sauce

2 tablespoons oil
1–2 cloves garlic, chopped finely
salt and pepper
2–3 tablespoons grated cheese

Heat the oil in a frying pan and fry the garlic until it just turns golden, do not let it burn or it will have a bitter flavour. Pile on to the drained pasta, season with the salt and pepper and sprinkle over the cheese.

Chicken liver sauce

1 tablespoon oil
1 onion, chopped
1 clove garlic, chopped
100 g (4 oz) chicken livers, sliced

Heat the oil in a frying pan and add the chopped onion, let it soften for a minute or two before adding the garlic and the chicken livers. Cook them gently over a low heat, turning them over from time to time for about 10 minutes. Pile on to the pasta which has already been mixed with oil or butter and seasoned with salt and pepper.

Mince sauce

Mince could be described as the meat-eating student's best buy. It is cheap and easy to cook although it is worth remembering that the very cheapest kind has a high proportion of fat which simply melts away as it is cooked, so it is actually more economical to spend a little more on low-fat mince. If you have no fridge, buy it the day you intend to eat it, otherwise refrigerate it for no more than 24 hours. It stores well in a freezer and, because it is free-flow, you can take out just what you need. You can cook it from frozen, making sure it is thoroughly browned and cooked before you eat it.

Beef is the most readily obtainable mince but you may come across minced pork and lamb and some supermarkets are now selling minced venison, which is very low in fat and an excellent buy.

The following recipe is mince at its simplest but it can be varied in countless ways and there are some ideas below.

$^1\!/_2$ tablespoon oil
100 g (4 oz) mince
1 small onion, chopped
1 clove garlic, chopped, optional
1 teaspoon tomato purée or $^1\!/_2$ teaspoon soy sauce
4 tablespoons stock or water
$^1\!/_4$ teaspoon dried mixed herbs
salt and pepper

Heat the oil in a frying pan, saucepan or wok and add the mince. Stir over a medium heat until it is brown all over. Add the chopped onion and garlic, mix well and continue to cook for 3–4 minutes. Stir in the tomato purée or soy sauce and the water. Season with the dried herbs, a pinch of salt and some pepper. Bring to the boil, cover, lower the heat and simmer for 15–20 minutes.

Variations to the above mince sauce

The following variations are just suggestions. You should try experimenting and inventing your own. Herbs can be varied and the dish can be spiced up by adding things like nutmeg, cumin, coriander, or what you will. The only rule is not to confuse the flavours by adding too many different kinds.

- *Dried fruit and nuts* – stir in a tablespoon of any kind of dried fruit or nuts to the finished dish and let it simmer for a further 5 minutes.
- *Pulses* – almost any kind of dried beans will increase the nutritional value of the basic recipe as well as adding flavour. Stir in $\frac{1}{2}$ can or $\frac{1}{2}$ mug cooked beans once all the other ingredients have been added, cover the pan and leave it to simmer for the specified time.
- *Pesto* – stir in 1 tablespoon to the finished dish.
- *Tomatoes, canned* – omit the water but add instead $\frac{1}{2}$ can Italian chopped tomatoes.
- *Vegetables* – all sorts of fresh vegetables will add interest and bulk to the basic recipe. Chop or slice them and add them once the onion and garlic have been fried. Let them cook and soften a little before stirring in the tomato purée and continuing with the recipe. Choose things like courgettes, mushrooms, carrots, sweet peppers, tomatoes, aubergines, potato and leeks.

Tuna sauce

1 can tuna in oil
1 onion, chopped
1 tablespoon tomato purée

Drain the oil from the can into a saucepan and heat it. Add the chopped onion and let it soften over a medium heat for 3–4 minutes. Add the tuna and tomato purée and stir until the sauce is piping hot. Pile on to the pasta which has already been mixed with oil or butter and seasoned with salt and pepper.

Follow this recipe using other kinds of canned fish like mussels, sardines, pilchards or cockles. Some of these are canned in brine, so you may have to use a tablespoon of oil to fry the onion.

Broccoli and garlic sauce

2 tablespoons oil
100 g (4 oz) fresh broccoli, cut in small pieces
1 clove garlic, chopped
2–3 tablespoons grated cheese

Heat the oil in a frying pan and gently fry the broccoli and garlic together for 10 minutes, turning the broccoli over from time to time. Pile on to the pasta which has already been mixed with oil or butter and seasoned with salt and pepper.

All sorts of other vegetables can be used in place of the broccoli, for example courgettes, cauliflower, sweet peppers, fennel, aubergines, chicory, mushrooms or a mixture of stir-fried vegetables. Whatever you decide to use, slice or chop them finely.

Tomato sauce

1 tablespoon oil
1 onion, chopped
1 clove garlic chopped, optional
1 can Italian chopped tomatoes
$^1/_2$ teaspoon dried oregano or marjoram
salt and pepper

Heat the oil in a saucepan and add the chopped onion, let it cook gently for about 5 minutes. Add the garlic, tomatoes and herbs. Season with salt and pepper. Stir and simmer, uncovered for 15–20 minutes, stirring occasionally to make sure the sauce does not burn. Pile on to the pasta which has already been mixed with oil or butter and seasoned with salt and pepper.

Once this sauce is cooked it can be varied by including any of the following:

- *Fish* – stir in and heat through the contents of either a can of anchovies, tuna, sardines, pilchards, mussels or prawns.
- *Meat* – add two or three rashers chopped bacon or 100 g (4 oz) of mince or chopped chicken livers (frying and browning them with the onion when you prepare your tomato sauce) or a slice or two of chopped cooked ham, salami or other Continental sausage.
- *Pulses* – stir in the contents of a can of chickpeas, sweetcorn, cannellini, flageolet or other pulses and heat through.
- *Vegetables* – add sliced courgettes, aubergines, mushrooms or sweet pepper (frying them with the onion when you prepare your tomato sauce).

Rice and other grains

Rice and other grains can be used in the same way as pasta as a base for two-pan meals and they can be eaten with many of the ideas and sauces given in the pasta section, or combined with eggs, vegetables or pulses.

When buying rice, go for varieties like American long-grained, patna or basmati and, for added nutrition, choose brown rice which hasn't been subjected to the same refining processes. It does take longer to cook but has a strong and pleasant nutty flavour.

Boiled rice

Boiling rice is easy and you don't need any sophisticated measuring devices, simply allow $\frac{1}{2}$ mug of rice per person.

1 mug water
pinch salt
$\frac{1}{2}$ mug white or brown rice

Boil the water in a saucepan, stir in the salt and rice. As soon as the water returns to the boil, reduce the heat to the lowest possible setting, cover the pan and simmer for 20 minutes for white rice and 40 minutes for brown. Turn off the heat and leave 5–10 minutes before removing the lid and serving.

Rice pilaff

If you happen to have an onion on hand, plain boiled rice can be turned into something a little more exciting.

1 tablespoon oil
1 small onion, chopped
water, salt and rice as in above recipe

Heat the oil in a saucepan and fry the chopped onion until soft, 3–4 minutes. Stir in the rice and continue to cook until it begins to turn opaque. Add the water and salt, bring to the boil, stir well and reduce the heat to the lowest possible setting, cover the pan and simmer for 20 minutes for white rice and 40 minutes for brown. Turn off the heat and leave 5–10 minutes before removing the lid and serving.

Other grains

As a change from rice use other grains like bulgar wheat, buckwheat, millet and couscous sold in health stores and some supermarkets. They are all quick to cook and each has its own distinctive flavour.

Bulgar wheat

Because the whole grain has already been boiled, dried and cracked, all you have to do is to steep bulgar wheat in boiling water.

$1/_2$ mug bulgar wheat
$3/_4$ mug boiling water
$1/_4$ teaspoon salt or 1 teaspoon soy sauce

Put the wheat into a bowl, pour over the water and stir in the salt or soy sauce. Cover the bowl and leave for 10–15 minutes. The grain will swell and absorb the water.

Buckwheat, millet and couscous

Cook these grains exactly like rice but allow the following quantities:

$1/_2$ mug buckwheat to $1 1/_2$ mugs water
$1/_2$ mug millet to $1 1/_2$ mugs water and increase cooking time by
  5 minutes
$1/_2$ mug couscous to 1 mug water

Left-over cooked rice and other grains

Don't throw away any left-over rice or other grains but use them as a base for another meal, though it's important to store them covered in the fridge because left to stand around for any length of time they can be a breeding ground for bacteria.

Try them in salad, mixed with your chosen dressing while still warm so the grains absorb the flavours (see page 138), or they can be fried quite simply in a little oil until piping hot.

Stir-fried rice or grains

If you have a wok, it is ideal for this type of quick frying and is a perfect way to turn a mugful of cooked grains into a filling meal.

You can add almost any kind of vegetable from frozen peas to green peppers, courgettes, mushrooms, tomatoes, carrots, beans, broccoli, cauliflower, whatever takes your fancy, and if you happen to have a piece of root ginger on hand, add a sliver finely chopped. The secret is to make sure that those vegetables that need chopping are cut into very small pieces.

2 tablespoons oil
1 onion, chopped
2 rashers of bacon, chopped
2–3 tablespoons chopped vegetables
1 egg, optional
1 mug cooked rice or other grain
few drops soy sauce

Heat 1 tablespoon of oil in a wok or frying pan and fry the onion and bacon and chopped vegetables until beginning to crisp. Push them to one side, add the remaining oil and break in the egg, if using. Stir quickly to mix and let it begin to set. Stir in the rice or other grain, sprinkle in the soy sauce, cover the pan and let everything cook over a low heat for several minutes until piping hot.

The whole thing can be made into more of a meal by leaving out the bacon and using mince or cooked chicken or ham, cut into small pieces. If using mince make sure it is thoroughly browned and cooked by letting it cook over a low heat for 10–15 minutes after the initial quick frying before adding the egg and other ingredients.

Pancakes

Pancakes with a savoury filling, topped with grated cheese are a delicious way of stretching limited ingredients into a full-sized meal, especially if eaten with something like baked jacket potatoes. Look out for ready-cooked pancakes sold in supermarkets or make your own either by using a batter-mix or by mixing your own batter. (Cooked pancakes keep for up to a week in the fridge provided they are covered, so you might consider doubling the quantity.)

Pancake batter – makes 5–6 pancakes

50 g (2 oz, 6 level tablespoons) plain flour
pinch salt
1 egg
150 ml ($^1/_4$ pint, 8 tablespoons) mixture of half milk and half water
1 teaspoon oil

Put the flour and salt into a bowl, make a hollow in the centre into which you break the egg.

Add 2 tablespoons of the liquid and begin to mix in the flour, gradually add the remaining milk and the water until all the flour is incorporated. The mixture should resemble thin cream without any lumps. Beat it well, using a whisk or wooden spoon, until it is frothy. Set aside for at least 30 minutes before using, to allow the flour to absorb the liquid. Just before using, add the oil and beat well again.

To cook the pancakes use a small frying pan, about 18 cm (7 in) diameter. Heat the pan over a medium heat and when it is hot grease it with the merest smear of oil. Pour 2 tablespoons of the batter into the pan and tilt it, using a circular motion, so that the batter runs completely over the base. It should be very thin. If holes appear, dribble in a little batter to cover. Let the pancake cook for 30–60 seconds until the surface is opaque and begins to blister.

Use a spatula to lift the edge, and when the base is golden turn the pancake over. Cook for a further 20 seconds or so, by which time the other side will be brown. Remove from the pan and make the remaining pancakes in the same way, stacking them on a plate as you go.

Pancake fillings

Pancakes can be filled with all sorts of fillings. You could use a ready-prepared pasta sauce, which you will find sold in supermarkets and smaller shops. Or make your own sauce. The one below uses mince which could be either beef, lamb, pork or even venison which is now sold in some supermarkets.

2 tablespoons of oil
1 onion, chopped
100 g (4 oz) mince
1 clove garlic, chopped – optional
1 can Italian chopped tomatoes
salt and pepper
$\frac{1}{4}$ teaspoon dried mixed herbs or oregano
1–2 tablespoons grated cheese

Heat half the oil (using the same frying pan in which you cooked the pancakes). Add the onion and fry until soft. Stir in the mince and continue to cook for a few minutes until it is brown all over. Stir in the garlic and chopped tomatoes, bring to the boil, season with salt, pepper and the mixed herbs or oregano. Simmer uncovered for 10–15 minutes, stirring occasionally to make sure it does not burn.

Instead of mince you could use any of the following: finely chopped chicken breast, chicken livers or bacon; or something like chopped, cooked ham, chicken or Continental sausage. For a vegetarian filling use sliced fried mushrooms, aubergines, courgettes or sweet peppers, or almost any kind of canned beans or a mix of stir-fried vegetables.

Assembling pancake dishes

Rub a little oil over a shallow oven-proof dish and either put a tablespoon or so of hot filling on each pancake, roll them up and lay them side by side in the dish, or lay the pancakes flat on top of each other in the dish, sandwiching each layer with a tablespoon or two of the filling.

Heat the pancakes either by putting them under the grill on the lowest possible rung until they are hot through and the cheese is melting and browned or put them into an oven heated to Gas 6–7/400–425°F/200–220°C for 10–15 minutes.

Sweet pancakes

Pancakes can also be filled with sweet fillings. The classic example is the kind we eat on Shrove Tuesdays, when they are sprinkled with lemon juice and sugar, before being rolled up and served immediately. Other fillings might include:

- *Banana* – slice up a banana and put on to the pancake with a tablespoon of marmalade, roll up and serve.
- *Fruit* – use fruit like apples and pears, slice them and fry them gently in a little oil or butter before putting them into the centre of a pancake, rolling up and serving.
- *Jam, marmalade* or *honey* – put a tablespoon of one of these in the centre of each pancake before rolling up and serving.
- *Spreads* – put a tablespoon of chocolate, chestnut or chocolate hazelnut spread on each pancake, before rolling up and serving.

Mashed potato base

Mashed potatoes make a good base for several dishes (including pizza, see page 93). They are nicest if freshly made but if time presses you could cheat a little by using a packet of instant potato mix.

350 g (12 oz) potatoes
salt and pepper
25 g (1 oz) butter or margarine
1 tablespoon milk

Put the peeled potatoes into a saucepan, cover them with water and bring to the boil with the lid on the pan. Add a pinch of salt, lower the heat and simmer until they are soft, about 20 minutes. Drain them well and mash using a fork, potato masher or even a bottle, until there are no more lumps. Season to taste with salt and pepper and mix in the butter and milk to make a creamy mixture.

They can be eaten with many of the sauces given in the pasta section or used as a base for the following dishes.

Bangers and mash

A really well-made sausage is something to be prized and occasionally it is worth splashing out on those sold by a reliable butcher or in specialist sausage shops. However, this is a counsel of perfection. Mass-produced sausages become more interesting if cooked with a finely sliced onion or a quartered apple, as in the recipe below.

1 tablespoon oil
1 onion, finely sliced, or 1 crisp eating apple, quartered and cored
100 g (4 oz) pork sausages
mashed potatoes, as above

Heat the oil in a frying pan and add the onion or apple and the sausages. Fry over a medium heat, turning the sausages until they are brown all over. Cover the pan, either with a lid or a piece of foil, lower the heat and let the sausages cook slowly for about 15–20 minutes. Serve them on top of the mashed potatoes.

Smoked sausages with mash

Smoked sausages like frankfurters are also delicious with mashed potatoes. Simply put them into a pan of boiling water and let them just simmer for 10–15 minutes; avoid letting the water boil fiercely because they will split and burst.

Tuna pie

This is a real nursery dish, delicious and simple to make. It consists of mashed potatoes mixed with a can of tuna fish, flavoured with tomatoes, all baked together in the oven until the top is bubbling and golden.

4–6 tablespoons mashed potato
225 g (8 oz) can tuna fish
3 or 4 sun-dried tomatoes chopped or 1 tablespoon tomato purée
salt and pepper
little butter or margarine

Mix the mashed potato with the tuna fish and sun-dried tomatoes or tomato purée. Season with salt and pepper. Turn the mixture into a shallow oven-proof dish, spread it evenly and make a criss-cross pattern all over the top with the prongs of a fork. Dot with the remaining butter or margarine cut in small pieces. Put into the oven heated to Gas 6/400°F/200°C for 25 minutes until hot through and golden.

Meat hash

1 tablespoon oil
1 onion, chopped
2–3 tablespoons cooked ham or chicken or corned beef
4 tablespoons mashed potatoes

pinch mixed herbs, optional
salt and pepper

Heat the oil in a frying pan. When it is hot, fry the chopped onion until it is soft. Mix the meat with the potato and mixed herbs. Add the mixture to the pan, spreading it evenly and press it well down to cover the base of the pan. Cook over a medium heat until the underside is golden brown, about 5 minutes. Using a spatula, turn the hash over. It doesn't matter if it breaks up, simply press it well down again and cook the other side until it is crisp and golden. Season to taste with salt and pepper.

Fish cakes

Fish cakes can be made from left-over fish or almost any kind of canned, such as tuna, sardines, salmon or pilchards.

$1/2$ mug left-over cooked fish or equivalent canned
$1/2$ mug mashed potato
1 teaspoon onion, finely chopped
few drops of lemon juice
salt and pepper
a little milk
1 tablespoon flour
1 tablespoon oil

Mix the fish with the potato and onion and season with lemon juice and salt and pepper. Mix in just sufficient milk to bind the mixture. Dampen your hands, to prevent the mixture sticking, and form it into two flat cakes. Put the flour on a plate and coat the fish cakes on both sides. (If you have no flour, don't worry, but take extra care when cooking that the fish cakes do not stick.) Set aside for 15 minutes or so to firm up.

Heat the oil in a frying pan over a medium heat. When it is hot, add the fish cakes. Cook briskly, turning once until both sides are golden, 5–10 minutes.

Liver and onions with mashed potatoes

This and the following recipe for *Kidneys with mustard* go particularly well with mashed potatoes but you could also eat them with pasta, rice or any other sort of grain. Lamb's liver is relatively cheap and cooked this way is soft and tender. You could stir in a teaspoon of tomato purée and finish it off by adding a tablespoon of plain yogurt.

1 tablespoon oil
1 onion, sliced
1 teaspoon sugar
100 g (4 oz) lamb's liver
salt and pepper
1/4 teaspoon mixed herbs
1 tablespoon water
mashed potato

Heat the oil in a frying pan or wok and when it is hot add the chopped onion and sugar (the sugar helps the onion to brown). Fry it until it is brown, 5–10 minutes. Meanwhile, cut the liver into very thin strips. Add to the pan and cook very briskly, turning the meat over, for 2–3 minutes. Add a pinch of salt, some pepper and the mixed herbs and stir in the water. Serve on top of the mashed potato.

Kidneys with mustard

The kidneys must have the outer fat and membrane removed. The butcher will do this for you, but if you buy them pre-packed, you might find there is still a thin skin surrounding them. It will come away quite easily if you first slit it with a pointed knife. Cut each kidney in half lengthways and cut out the small core of fat in the centre – use scissors. Cut each half into two or three slices.

1 tablespoon oil
2 lamb's kidneys
1 teaspoon made mustard
salt and pepper
1 tablespoon plain yogurt
mashed potato

Heat the oil in a frying pan or wok and when it is hot add the slices of kidney. Cook them gently for 5–10 minutes, turning them over from time to time. Stir in the mustard, season with salt and pepper and stir in the yogurt. Serve on top of the mashed potato.

Add a few drops of Worcester sauce if you have any, or vary the dish by frying a chopped onion before frying the kidneys. A few sliced mushrooms or a chopped tomato can be added when the kidneys are cooked: stir-fry over a high heat for 2–3 minutes before adding the seasonings.

Bubble and squeak

This is a real dish of left-overs using mashed potato mixed with chopped cooked greens, all fried until golden brown. It is delicious eaten on its own or with sausages, baked beans or eggs and bacon.

1 tablespoon oil
3–4 tablespoons mashed potatoes
2–3 tablespoons left-over greens, chopped
salt and pepper
pinch of ground nutmeg, optional

Heat the oil in a frying pan until it just begins to foam. Mix the potatoes and greens together and put the mixture into the pan, pressing it down well to cover the base evenly. Cook over a medium heat until the bottom is crisp and brown, about 5–10 minutes. Season with salt and pepper and a pinch of nutmeg.

Quiches

Ready-made quiches, savoury flans with a pastry base, are widely available and provide a quick base for a meal, but not surprisingly it is cheaper to make your own. You will need a flan tin measuring 18 cm (7 in), preferably one with a removable base, which will provide two servings. If pastry-making is not for you, buy it ready-made either fresh or frozen, or use a mix. Any left-over pastry can be rolled into a ball and stored in a plastic bag in the fridge for two or three days or, if it has not already been frozen, in the freezer.

In fact, if time is really pressing you can do without the pastry altogether by simply cooking the filling in a well-greased oven dish, when you'll have achieved a gratin rather than a quiche. Cook it in a pre-heated oven, Gas 5/375°F/190°C for 15–20 minutes until it is puffed and golden. (The dish can be a bit of a pain to wash up but a trick to shift even the most stubborn burnt-on bits is to fill the offending pan with very hot water with a tablespoon or two of washing soda thrown in, leave it to soak overnight and it will wash like a dream next day.)

Shortcrust pastry

The following method is slightly unconventional but it has the merit of being quick. You must use the kind of fat labelled for baking, either a soft margarine or one of the white pastry fats.

150 g (6 oz, 1 mug) plain flour
pinch salt
approximately 2 tablespoons cold water
75 g (3 oz) either soft margarine or white pastry fat, cut in small pieces

Put about one third of the flour and the salt into a bowl and make a hollow in the middle. Add 1 tablespoon of the water and the fat cut in small pieces. Mash with a fork to make a creamy mixture. Stir in the rest of the flour and mix together, adding just sufficient water

97

to form a firm dough. Sprinkle your hands with flour and form the dough into a ball; put it into a plastic bag and leave it in the fridge for half an hour before using. (This allows the dough to shrink before it is rolled, otherwise it tends to shrink when cooking.)

To roll out, sprinkle the work surface and the rolling pin with flour, flatten the ball of dough with the heel of your hand and roll it into a rough circle slightly larger than the flan tin, using light strokes and turning the dough as necessary. If it sticks, sprinkle a little more flour on the work surface. Fold the circle in half, lift it carefully and lay it over one side of the tin, flip it over to cover the base. Ease it to fit, working outwards and pressing it lightly against the sides of the tin. Take the rolling pin across the top edge to cut away surplus dough.

Quiche fillings

Basically the filling consists of a base of vegetables, meat or fish topped with eggs, milk or cream, often flavoured with cheese, which are beaten together to form a smooth custard. It comes from the oven all puffed and golden, when it is at its most delicious. Once cold the filling settles and won't rise again even if reheated.

18 cm (7 in) flan tin lined with pastry
2 eggs
6 tablespoons either single cream or milk or a mixture of milk and
    curd cheese
salt and pepper
filling – see below
1–2 tablespoons grated cheese, optional

Heat the oven to Gas 5/375°F/190°C. Beat the eggs in a bowl with either the single cream or milk or the mixture of milk and curd cheese. Season with salt and pepper and add the pinch of nutmeg. Lay your choice of filling over the pastry base, pour over the egg mixture and sprinkle over the grated cheese if using. Bake for 25–30 minutes until puffed and golden.

Ideas for quiche fillings

- *Bacon* – cut 3 or 4 rashers into small pieces and fry until crisp without any oil or fat. For extra interest, add a chopped onion or a sliced leek and a tablespoon of oil and fry with the bacon.
- *Broccoli* – divide into florets and boil or steam them until beginning to soften, 5–10 minutes.
- *Canned vegetables* – for quick quiches buy asparagus pieces, sweetcorn, spinach, chopped tomatoes, mushrooms etc. Drain them well and mix with the egg mixture before pouring over the pastry base.
- *Cheese* – grate 50–75 g (2–3 oz) and stir half into the mixture, sprinkle the rest on top.
- *Chicken livers* – use 50–75 g (2–3 oz) cut in small pieces and fry them in a little oil with a chopped onion until the livers are brown all over and the onion softened. (Chicken livers are sold frozen in 225 g (8 oz) tubs. Let them defrost thoroughly before using and store the left-overs, covered in the fridge, to be used the next day; see index for ideas.)
- *Ham* – cut a slice or two of ham into small pieces and mix it with a sliced banana or a chopped onion or a sliced leek fried in a little oil until soft.
- *Mushrooms* – chop 50–75 g (2–3 oz) mushrooms and a small onion and fry them gently until soft in a little oil.
- *Onion* – chop or slice 2 onions and fry them gently in a little oil until soft, about 15 minutes.
- *Spinach* – wash 100 g (4 oz) and cook it in a saucepan with no added water until it shrinks, 2 or 3 minutes. Drain very well. Wipe out the saucepan and fry a chopped onion for a few minutes. Mix with the spinach.
- *Tomato* – slice 2 or 3 tomatoes, sprinkle them with a little salt and set aside for 30 minutes to exude their liquid. Dry them with kitchen paper and lay them flat on the pastry base with a sprinkling of dried basil or oregano.

- *Tuna and tomato* – prepare tomatoes as above, break up the contents of a small can of tuna, add to the egg mixture and pour over the tomatoes.

Group cooking

Ways with mince
Casseroles
Chicken dinners
Fish dishes
That Sunday roast

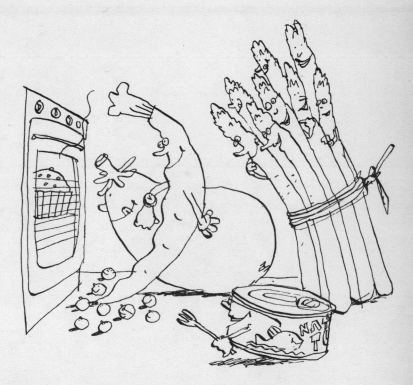

There are going to be times when you'll want to cook for more than yourself or maybe you're one of a group who wants to share the cooking. Lots of the recipes in the other sections of the book can of course be adapted to fit the bill by doubling or trebling the quantities or whatever, depending on the numbers you're catering for. The only thing which doesn't quite follow that rule is the use of seasonings such as salt, pepper, herbs and spices. How much extra to add depends on your own sense of taste, which in any case you should always rely on.

Ways with mince

Mince is a great standby. It's reasonably cheap and easy to cook and can be used in a variety of dishes. As well as beef, look out for lamb, pork and venison. This latter is very lean and excellent value. Don't necessarily buy the cheapest mince, which can be full of fat.

Bolognese sauce – serves 4

An old favourite which is ideal for feeding a group. Serve it with long *spaghetti* or *tagliatelle* allowing 75–100g (3–4 oz) per head (see page 79) and hand round a bowl of grated cheese – or just hand the cheese in a lump with the cheese grater and get everyone to grate their own.

1 tablespoon oil
1 onion, chopped
350 g (12 oz) mince
1 clove garlic, chopped
1 medium can Italian chopped tomatoes
½ teaspoon dried oregano, marjoram or basil
salt and pepper

Heat the oil in a saucepan and fry the onion for a few minutes until soft. Stir in the mince and garlic and continue to cook until the meat is brown all over, stirring all the time. Mix in the can of tomatoes, add the dried oregano, marjoram or basil and season to taste with salt and pepper. Lower the heat and cook the sauce, uncovered, for 15–20 minutes. Stir it occasionally to make sure it does not burn.

For a more substantial sauce once the meat has browned, add a few chopped mushrooms and perhaps a green or red pepper. On lean days substitute some of the mince with a can or mugful of any cooked pulses, stirring this in at the same time as the tomatoes. (You can make the same sauce using canned tuna which doesn't need browning but is added with the tomatoes and other ingredients.)

Lasagne – serves 4

This is a great dish to feed lots of people, though it does take a certain amount of time to prepare, so don't decide to make it 30 minutes before you want to eat. You can even prepare it the day before and let it cool before storing it, covered, in the fridge. If you decide to do this and use an earthenware dish, put it into a cold oven because if it goes straight from the fridge to a hot one, the dish might crack.

Like most traditional recipes, there are many different versions. In this recipe, the dish consists of pasta sheets – lasagne – sandwiched between layers of the above *Bolognese* sauce. It is topped with a cheese sauce, which can be the cooked one given on page 144 or the simple uncooked sauce given below. To save on the amount of work, look out for the kind of lasagne that doesn't need a preliminary cooking: it is slightly more expensive but worth the extra pennies.

350 g (12 oz) ready-cooked or ordinary lasagne
Bolognese sauce as in recipe above
cheese sauce, see page 144 *or* uncooked cheese sauce:
   225 g (8 oz) curd cheese
   1 egg, beaten
   1–2 tablespoons milk
   salt and pepper
   2–3 tablespoons grated cheese

First prepare the lasagne and the Bolognese and cheese sauces. If making the uncooked cheese sauce, simply mix the curd cheese with the beaten egg, stir in the milk to make a thick but runny consistency and season with salt and pepper. (If you are using ordinary as opposed to ready-cooked sheets of lasagne, follow the instructions for cooking pasta on page 79.)

To assemble: Smear a little oil over a shallow oven dish. Spread about one third of the Bolognese sauce over the base, lay half the sheets of lasagne on top, overlapping them if necessary. Spread another third of the Bolognese sauce on top and lay the remaining sheets on top of that. Finish with a layer of Bolognese sauce. Pour over the cheese sauce, spreading it evenly and sprinkle over the grated cheese and dribble a little oil on top.

Bake in an oven heated to Gas 4/350°F/180°C for 50 minutes until the top is golden brown. (If you've stored the dish in the fridge, allow an extra 20–30 minutes.) Check half-way through and if the top is becoming too brown, cover the top with a piece of foil.

Moussaka – serves 4

This Greek dish is not so very different from the Italian *Lasagne*. It uses minced lamb and, instead of the pasta, the dish is topped with slices of aubergine which have been fried in oil. In place of aubergines, you could use courgettes or even sliced, cooked potatoes.

450 g (1 lb) aubergines, courgettes or potato
6 tablespoons oil
1 onion, chopped
350 g (12 oz) minced lamb
1 teaspoon plain flour
1 can Italian chopped tomatoes, drained
salt and pepper
1/2 teaspoon dried oregano or mixed herbs
1 carton thick Greek style yogurt
3 egg yolks
4 tablespoons grated cheese

Slice the aubergines or courgettes into rings, lay them on a board and sprinkle them with salt; this will release their juices and make them absorb less oil when they are fried. (If using potatoes, boil them in their skins until soft, about 20 minutes, and when cool enough to handle, cut in slices).

Meanwhile make the meat sauce by heating 2 tablespoons of oil in a saucepan and frying the chopped onion with the minced lamb until the onion begins to soften and the lamb is brown all over. Mix in the teaspoon of flour, the drained tomatoes and season with a little salt and pepper and the dried oregano or mixed herbs. Simmer for 10–15 minutes, uncovered, until the sauce is thick and nearly all the liquid from the tomatoes has evaporated.

While the sauce is simmering, rinse the aubergine or courgette slices to rid them of the salt and dry with kitchen paper. Heat the remaining oil in a wok or frying pan and fry the slices quickly on each side until beginning to brown. Drain on pieces of kitchen paper.

Beat the yogurt with the 3 egg yolks (to separate eggs, see page 159) and stir in 3 tablespoons of the grated cheese.

Heat the oven to Gas 5/375°F/190°C. In a shallow oven-proof dish put first a layer of aubergines, courgettes or potatoes, top with the meat sauce and cover with the remaining slices of vegetable. Pour the yogurt sauce over the top and sprinkle with the remaining grated cheese. Bake for 45 minutes.

Meatballs with yogurt – serves 4

450 g (1 lb) mince
1 clove garlic, finely chopped
1 small onion, finely chopped
6 tablespoons breadcrumbs
salt and pepper
$1/_2$ teaspoon dried mixed herbs
4 eggs
2 tablespoons plain flour
2 tablespoons oil
1 carton thick Greek style yogurt

Heat the oven to Gas 4/350°F/180°C. Mix the mince with the chopped garlic, onion and breadcrumbs. (Make breadcrumbs by grating stale bread, or soak fresh bread in a little milk or water, then squeeze it out before using.) Season with a little salt and pepper and the mixed herbs. Beat one of the eggs into the mixture. Put the flour on a plate and, using wet hands, divide the mixture into 12 pieces, rolling them into balls. Roll the balls in the flour to evenly coat them. Heat the oil in a wok or frying pan and brown the meatballs all over, transferring them to an oven-proof dish. Put the dish in the oven and bake for 30 minutes. Beat the remaining eggs with the yogurt and pour over the meatballs, return to the oven for 10–15 minutes.

Chilli con carne – serves 4

Serve this chilli with plain rice. It is garnished right at the end with chopped coriander leaves, which can be bought at ethnic shops and at some supermarkets and greengrocers. It adds a pleasant, bitter flavour.

2 tablespoons oil
1 onion, chopped
225 g (8 oz) mince
2 teaspoons chilli powder
1 tablespoon tomato purée
1 can Italian chopped tomatoes
1 can or cup of cooked red kidney beans
salt and pepper
2–3 tablespoons chopped coriander leaves, optional

Heat the oil in a large saucepan and fry the onion for a few minutes before stirring in the minced meat and frying it gently until it is brown all over. Stir in the chilli powder, tomato purée, the can of tomatoes and red kidney beans. Season with a little salt and pepper. Bring to the boil, put on the lid and simmer for 30–40 minutes. Sprinkle over the coriander before serving.

Meat loaf – serves 4

This dish takes only minutes to prepare. Make breadcrumbs by grating a piece of stale bread on a cheese grater or use rolled oats or cooked rice or other grains in their place. You can eke out the meat by halving the amount of mince and adding a mugful of canned or cooked pulses instead.

350 g (12 oz) mince
1 onion, finely chopped
4 tablespoons breadcrumbs
1 egg
4 tablespoons stock or water
1 teaspoon tomato purée
1 teaspoon soy sauce
salt and pepper
$\frac{1}{2}$ teaspoon mixed dried herbs

Heat oven to Gas 4/350°F/180°C. Grease a small loaf tin with a little oil, margarine or butter. Mix all the ingredients in a bowl and transfer them to the tin, smoothing the top evenly with the back of a spoon. Bake for 45 minutes. (If you haven't got a loaf tin, form the mixture into a loaf shape, wrap it in foil and put on a baking sheet.)

Stuffed vegetables – serves 4

Vegetables like sweet peppers, aubergines, courgettes, tomatoes, mushrooms and marrow lend themselves to stuffing and make wonderfully filling meals for a group. If you don't want to eat meat, you can use almost any kind of cooked pulses instead, and if you are tired of cheese, top the dish with chopped nuts or whole seeds such as sunflower, sesame or pumpkin.

1 tablespoon oil
225 g (8 oz) mince or a mixture of mince and cooked pulses
1 onion, chopped
1 can of Italian tomatoes

salt and pepper
clove of garlic, chopped
$^1/_2$ teaspoon dried mixed herbs
vegetable to be stuffed, see table below
2 or 3 tablespoons grated cheese

Heat the oil in a frying pan and fry the mince, turning it over and over until it is brown. Add the onion and fry for a few minutes longer. Mix in two or three of the canned tomatoes, a little salt and pepper, the garlic and herbs. Use this mixture to stuff your chosen vegetable.

Fill your chosen vegetable with the stuffing and pour the remaining tomatoes into an oven-proof dish or casserole. Lay the vegetables in the sauce, top with the grated cheese and bake for the specified time in an oven heated to Gas 5/375°F/190°C.

	Preparation	Cooking time
Aubergines	$^1/_2$ per person. Cut in half lengthways, scoop out the centre and mix with the stuffing. Fill the cavities.	45–60 minutes
Courgettes	1 per person. Prepare as aubergines.	30–40 minutes
Marrow	Choose one about 30 cm (12 in) long. Cut in half lengthways, scoop out and discard seeds with a spoon. Boil the 2 halves in salted water for 5 minutes. Fill the halves and bind together with string.	1 hour or until the marrow is soft when pierced with a pointed knife.
Mushrooms	1 or 2 large flat per person. Remove stalks, chop and add to basic stuffing and fill cavities	15–20 minutes

(contd over)

	Preparation	Cooking time
Sweet peppers	1 per person. Cut off stalk end, scoop out seeds and boil the peppers for 5 minutes in boiling, salted water. Fill the cavities.	30–40 minutes
Tomatoes	1 or 2 per head. Cut in half, scoop out flesh and seeds and mix with the basic mince stuffing.	15–20 minutes

Cottage pie – serves 4

Traditionally this was made from the minced left-over remains of the Sunday joint (beef for *Cottage pie* and lamb for *Shepherd's pie*). There's no reason why you can't use fresh mince. Follow the recipe for the filling for the stuffed vegetables, see above, but use the whole, drained can of tomatoes and a $\frac{1}{2}$ teaspoon of soy or Worcester sauce. Spread the mixture into a shallow oven-proof dish. Top with a layer of mashed potatoes, see page 92, using about 700 g ($1\frac{1}{2}$ lbs) or use a packet of *instant mash*. Mark the surface all over with the prongs of a fork and dot with small pieces of butter. Put under a hot grill to brown for 5–10 minutes, or if re-heating from cold, put into a pre-heated oven Gas 6/400°F/200°C for 25–30 minutes.

Stuffed pitta bread – serves 4

In too much of a hurry to stuff vegetables or make cottage pie? Make the sauce and simmer it until almost all the liquid has evaporated and use it to stuff pieces of pitta bread, cut crosswise. They open out to form a pocket. This is even nicer if you add 1 or 2 tablespoons of dried mixed fruit and season the sauce with $\frac{1}{2}$ teaspoon cinnamon and a little thyme.

Red dragon pie – serves 4

Strictly speaking this recipe has no place here as it contains no meat but it seems appropriate to include it because it is a sort of vegetarian version of cottage pie. It is made from a combination of aduki beans and brown rice. If you don't want to make mashed potatoes, top it instead with a mixture of 2 or 3 tablespoons wheatgerm and an equal amount of grated cheese, sprinkled with a few sesame seeds or chopped nuts.

1 tablespoon oil
1 onion, chopped
1 clove garlic, chopped
1 teaspoon sesame seeds
$\frac{1}{2}$ teaspoon cumin
1 mug brown rice
1 can or 1 mug cooked aduki beans
600 ml (1 pint, 2 mugs) water
salt and pepper
700 g (1$\frac{1}{2}$ lbs) mashed potatoes
25 g (1 oz) butter or margarine

Heat the oil in a saucepan and fry the onion and garlic for a few minutes. Add the sesame seeds and cumin and let them just sizzle. Stir in the rice and mix until every grain is coated. Add the aduki beans and the water and season with salt and pepper. Stir well and bring to the boil. Cover the pan, lower the heat and simmer gently for 40 minutes. Remove from the heat and leave to stand for 10 minutes.

Assemble the pie by putting the rice and bean mixture into a shallow oven-proof dish, smooth over the mashed potatoes and mark the surface with the prongs of a fork. Dot with small pieces of butter or margarine. Brown under a hot grill for 5–10 minutes or in an oven heated to Gas 5/375°F/190°C for 25–30 minutes.

Casseroles

Casseroles make perfect one-pot meals for a group. They were devised by people with very limited cooking facilities, just a pot suspended over the fire, and used whatever happened to be to hand and in season at that moment. Everything slowly simmers together until all the flavours are released and all the contents are meltingly tender.

Casseroles can be cooked on top of the stove or in the oven. The ideal pot to use for either method is a heavy-based, enamelled, cast-iron one but these are prohibitively expensive. Keep your eyes skinned at boot-sales and in charity shops or persuade a relative to buy or lend you one. Earthenware is much cheaper and is excellent for oven cooking but, whatever some makers claim, can't be used with total peace of mind on top of the stove.

There are two basic ways to prepare a casserole. One is to put everything into the pot and let it all cook together, the other is to pre-fry meat and vegetables so that they are browned and sealed and retain all their juices. Below are some examples of each.

Hot pot – serves 4

This Lancashire dish is closely related to the famous Irish stew. Lamb chops and kidneys are layered with onions, mushrooms and potatoes and allowed to stew gently until all the flavours mingle into a filling dish. It's assembled in minutes but needs 2½–3 hours to cook.

900 g (2 lbs) potatoes, sliced
8 neck of lamb chops, trimmed of most of the fat
4 lamb's kidneys, cut in half
450 g (1 lb) onions, sliced
100 g (4 oz) mushrooms
1 teaspoon mixed herbs

salt and pepper
300 ml (½ pint) stock or water + stock cube
25 g (1 oz) margarine or butter

Heat the oven to Gas 3/325°F/160°C. Lay half the potatoes over the base of a deep casserole and cover with layers of chops, kidneys, onions and mushrooms, sprinkling in a little of the mixed herbs and adding a little salt and pepper as each layer is made. Make a final layer with the remaining potatoes, pour in the stock or water and crumble in the stock cube if using. Dot with the margarine or butter cut in small pieces. Cover and put into the oven for 2½–3 hours. Remove the lid during the last 30 minutes to allow the top layer of potatoes to brown.

Pork chops with potatoes – serves 4

In this French recipe chops and onions are first browned in a little oil before being cooked on top of a dish of sliced potatoes. This same recipe can be used for lamb chops.

2 tablespoons oil
4 pork shoulder chops
2 onions, chopped
900 g (2 lbs) potatoes, peeled and sliced
½ teaspoon dried mixed herbs
2 cloves garlic, chopped
salt and pepper
8 rashers streaky bacon
water

Heat the oil in a frying pan and brown the chops quickly on both sides, remove to a plate. Add the onions to the pan and let them fry gently while you peel the potatoes and cut them in thin slices. Put half the potatoes in an oven-proof dish or large casserole and top with half the onions. Lay the chops on top and cover with remaining potatoes and onions. Sprinkle in the mixed herbs and garlic and season with a little salt and pepper. Lay the rashers of bacon over the top. Pour over sufficient water barely to cover. Heat the oven to Gas 6/400°F/200°C and bake for 1 hour until the potatoes are soft.

Sausages in beer – serves 4

Beer, sausages, potatoes and apples merge their flavours in this bitter-sweet dish based on a recipe from northern France. Don't begrudge the beer, it really does make all the difference.

4 tablespoons oil
450 g (1 lb) sausages
900 g (2 lbs) potatoes, peeled and thinly sliced
450 g (1 lb) hard eating apples
salt and pepper
200 ml (7 fl oz) light beer

Heat the oven to Gas 5/375°F/190°C. Heat the oil in a flame-proof casserole and fry the sausages quickly all over until beginning to brown. Add the sliced potatoes and fry them for a few minutes, turning them over and over. Quarter and core the apples and add to the pan, season with a little salt and pepper and pour over the beer. Cover with the lid and put into the oven for 40 minutes. (If your casserole is not flame-proof, do the preliminary frying in a frying pan, transferring everything to your casserole as you go.)

Rabbit in bacon – serves 4

Rabbit is relatively cheap. You can buy it ready-jointed or as frozen cubes in many supermarkets and the wild variety is much cheaper than tame. This recipe could also be used using small pieces of jointed chicken.

2 tablespoons oil
1 large onion, chopped
8 rabbit joints
salt and pepper

8 rashers streaky bacon
1 can Italian chopped tomatoes
$\frac{1}{2}$ teaspoon dried herbs
4 cloves garlic

Heat the oven to Gas 6/400°F/200°C. Heat the oil in a flame-proof casserole and fry the chopped onion for a few minutes until turning golden. Sprinkle each piece of rabbit with a little salt, pepper and dried herbs and wrap in a rasher of bacon. Pour the tomatoes over the onions, add the garlic, lay the rabbit pieces on top and bring to boiling point. Put into the oven for 45 minutes.

Chicken dinners

Chicken is one of the least expensive meats and can be cooked in many ways. If a recipe calls for it to be divided into portions, it's cheaper to buy a whole chicken and do this chore yourself. However, you may find it is worth paying for the time saved by buying chicken pieces.

Chicken kebabs – serves 4

Eat these kebabs with rice or other grains or simply with pitta or Naan bread and a simple salad.

450 g (1 lb) boned chicken thighs
lemon juice
pepper
1 teaspoon mixed dried herbs
1 clove garlic, chopped
1 sweet pepper
4 tomatoes
oil

Cut the chicken into bite-sized portions and put them in a china or glass bowl with the lemon juice, a seasoning of pepper, the herbs and garlic and set aside for at least 30 minutes. Cut the pepper and tomatoes into even-sized chunks. Thread the meat, pepper and tomatoes on to 4 skewers. Heat the grill and when it is very hot put the kebabs into the pan, sprinkle with a little oil and grill for 10–12 minutes, turning frequently until the meat and vegetables are browned and cooked.

Chicken sautéed

2 tablespoons oil
4 chicken leg joints
1 teaspoon dried mixed herbs

150 ml (¼ pint) stock or water + ½ stock cube
salt and pepper

Heat the oil in a pan and fry the chicken all over until it is golden
brown, doing it in two batches and setting aside on a plate. When
all the joints are brown, return them to the pan, sprinkle in the
mixed herbs, add the stock or water and ½ stock cube and season
with salt and pepper. Cover, lower the heat and simmer for 1 hour.

This is the simplest, most basic recipe for this type of dish. There
are dozens of variations such as adding a tablespoon or so of
tomato purée or a teaspoon of soy sauce, or adding some sun-dried
or fresh quartered tomatoes or a few mushrooms, and/or frying a
sliced onion or a chopped clove of garlic in the oil before returning
the browned chicken pieces. If you happen to have a little wine,
cider or even beer on hand, substitute this for the stock or water. If
you use cider, try frying a few slices of apple in the oil after browning the chicken and when they are soft, set the joints on top. They
melt to a smooth, sweet and delicious purée. If you can use fresh
herbs instead of the dried, by all means do so. Tarragon, oregano
and thyme are particularly successful.

Chicken with forty cloves of garlic – serves 4

This is the ultimate garlic dish and it comes from Provence. It
doesn't have to be exactly forty cloves, but go for as many as you
can. They are cooked whole in their skins and are eaten by pressing with a fork so that the soft centre oozes out. They taste sweet
and only slightly pungent. You'll need herbs too, preferably fresh,
but if you can't lay your hands on these, make do with dried.

1½ kg (3–3½ lb) chicken
salt and pepper
6 tablespoons oil
fresh sprigs of herbs like rosemary, thyme, sage, parsley or use dried
40 whole cloves of garlic, unpeeled
1 tablespoon flour and a little water

Use a casserole, earthenware is ideal. Put a little salt and pepper inside the chicken and a few sprigs of herbs or a sprinkling of dried. Pour the oil into the casserole and add more sprigs of herbs or a sprinkling of dried herbs and all the cloves of garlic. Lay the chicken on top and turn it over and over to coat it in the oil. Mix the flour with sufficient water to make a thick paste, and using your finger, smear it all round the inside edge of the lid. Put the lid on the pot, the paste will act as a seal so that no steam can escape. Put into the oven for 1½ hours. Bring the pot to the table so that the mingled smells of chicken, garlic and herbs are released as you lift the lid, needless to say using a cloth to protect your hand.

Chicken curry – serves 4

If you're keen on curry and Indian dishes, you'll probably want to try your hand at making your own. To be successful you'll need to invest in an assortment of spices: ready-mixed curry powder really doesn't have the authentic flavour. The following is simple to make and should be eaten with rice or Naan bread and perhaps some thinly sliced rings of raw onion and an Indian relish or one of the *raita* given below.

Curry improves with keeping, so if you like to be organized, make it a day ahead and reheat it just before serving, making sure it comes to the boil and then is simmered for 30 minutes.

2 tablespoons oil
1 onion, chopped
2 cloves garlic, chopped
thin sliver of root ginger, chopped
1 teaspoon chilli powder
1 teaspoon turmeric
1 teaspoon ground cumin
1 teaspoon ground coriander
4 chicken joints
can of Italian chopped tomatoes

lemon juice
salt

Heat the oil in a saucepan and fry the onion, garlic and ginger for a minute or two. Sprinkle in the chilli powder, turmeric, cumin and coriander and stir over a medium heat for 2 or 3 minutes. Add the chicken joints and mix well and continue to cook briskly for several minutes, turning the pieces over. Pour in the can of tomatoes, add a squeeze of lemon juice and a little salt. Bring to the boil. Cover the pan and leave to simmer slowly for 1–1½ hours.

Yogurt raita

These raitas are easy to make:

- *Banana* – allow ½ per person, slice and cover with plain yogurt flavoured with a pinch of powdered cumin.
- *Cucumber* – allow 1 tablespoon chopped cucumber per person, mix with plain yogurt and finely chopped onion or garlic.
- *Tomato* – allow 1 per head, slice and cover with plain yogurt flavoured with a pinch of powdered coriander.

Poppadums

Buy poppadums from Indian shops where they are cheaper than in supermarkets. They are sold in packets and need to be fried. Do this by heating a frying pan with about 1 cm (½ in) oil in the base. When it is just beginning to smoke, add one poppadum and cook over a high heat. Have 2 spatulas handy and use these to spread the poppadum outwards as it swells and crisps, then turn it over and cook for a further 30 seconds. Remove and drain it either on kitchen paper, or better still propped upright, perhaps in a toast rack. Repeat with remaining poppadums, allowing 1–2 per head. When the oil has cooled, discard it.

Some supermarkets sell packets of ready-fried poppadums, they're pricey but you might think them worth buying to save you some trouble.

Oven-fried chicken

This is a great way of cooking chicken, especially if at the same time you bake some jacket potatoes or other vegetable.

1–2 joints of chicken per person
lemon juice
pepper
1/2 teaspoon dried mixed herbs
1 clove garlic, chopped
oil
ready-made mustard, optional

Lay the chicken pieces in a shallow china or glass dish (not metal as this acts adversely with lemon juice). Sprinkle with a little lemon juice and pepper, the mixed herbs and chopped garlic. Set aside for 30 minutes to marinate. Heat the oven to Gas 7/425°F/220°C. Lay the chicken pieces in a single layer, skin side up, in a roasting tin or shallow oven-proof dish and sprinkle with the oil. Spread a little mustard on each, if using. Bake for 20 minutes. Remove from the oven, using a cloth, and spoon some of the hot oil over each piece. Return to the oven for 10–15 minutes until the chicken is done. Test by inserting a skewer into one: if the juice runs clear it is done, if pink it needs a little longer.

Roast chicken – serves 4

If you feel like a roast and you've several to cook for, chicken is your cheapest option. The least pricey is a frozen bird but it's worth too looking out for corn-fed chicken which is not that much dearer and has a much better flavour. If the bird has been frozen make sure it is thoroughly thawed before you cook it and that it has been out of the fridge for at least 30 minutes ahead of time, otherwise it will be tough.

Unless you're crazy about stuffing, you can do without this feature and fill the cavity with herbs and garlic, but if you insist on a touch of tradition, serve it with bread sauce which is very simple to make.

1½ kg (3–3½ lb) chicken
1 tablespoon butter or margarine
1 whole clove garlic
sprigs of rosemary or thyme or 1 teaspoon dried mixed herbs
3–4 tablespoons oil

Heat the oven to Gas 5/375°F/190°C. Put the chicken in a roasting tin and put the butter or margarine, clove of garlic and the herbs into the cavity. Pour over the oil. When the oven is hot, put the chicken on the centre shelf and roast for 20 minutes per 450 g (1 lb) + 20 minutes. Test the chicken is cooked by inserting a skewer into the thick part of the leg: if the juice runs pink, cook a little longer. Turn off the oven and leave the chicken to rest for 15 minutes before removing, which allows the meat to compact and makes it easier to carve.

Bread sauce

This is an unconventional but effective way of cooking bread sauce.

1 slice of bread 3.5 cm (1½ in) thick
300 ml (½ pint) milk
1 small onion
2 whole cloves, optional
salt and pepper

Put the bread and milk into a small saucepan. Stick the onion with the two whole cloves, if using, and add to the pan. Heat the pan over a low heat, breaking up the bread with a fork. Let it simmer for 5 minutes and add a little salt and pepper. Cover and set aside for 30 minutes to absorb the flavour of the onion. Just before serving, reheat over a low heat and remove the onion.

Pot-roasted chicken – serves 4

If you have no oven, you can pot-roast a chicken instead but you must have a heavy-based pan with a tight-fitting lid in which it will fit comfortably.

2 tablespoons oil
1½ kg (3–3½ lb) chicken
150 ml (¼ pint, ½ mug) stock or water + a stock cube
1 onion, chopped
1 carrot, chopped
salt and pepper
½ teaspoon mixed dried herbs

Heat the oil in a heavy-based pan on a medium heat and fry the chicken, turning it until it is brown all over. Lower the heat and pour in the stock (or the water and crumble in the stock cube). Add the onion and carrot, season with a little salt and pepper and the mixed herbs. Put on the lid and cook very gently allowing 30 minutes per 450 g (1 lb).

All sorts of cheap joints of meat like brisket of beef can be cooked following this method but will take longer to cook, around 45 minutes per 450 g (1 lb).

Chicken liver risotto – serves 4

Another good Italian standby to feed hungry appetites. This recipe uses rice and it's essential to make it with short-grain Italian rice which is rich and creamy. It calls for a well-flavoured stock which can happily be made using a stock cube.

The stock is added to the pan gradually as the rice absorbs the liquid, so it is a dish which needs to be tended carefully and is definitely something to make when you're in the mood for a bit of cooking and have friends to feed.

1 chicken stock cube
1 litre (1¾ pints, 4 mugs) boiling water
2 tablespoons oil
225 g (8 oz) chicken livers, chopped
1 onion, chopped
1 clove garlic, crushed
225 g (8 oz) mushrooms, sliced
350 g (12 oz, 1½ mugs) Italian rice
1 tablespoon tomato purée
50 g (2 oz) butter
salt and pepper
3–4 tablespoons grated cheese

Dissolve the stock cube in the boiling water and keep it hot. In a large, wide-mouthed saucepan, heat the oil and fry the chicken livers until brown all over, remove them on to a plate. Add the onion, garlic and mushrooms to the pan and cook them for several minutes, stirring. Add the rice, tomato purée and the browned chicken livers and mix well. Pour in about one-third of the stock, stir well, turn the heat low and let it all simmer uncovered. Watch it and as the water is absorbed so stir in more, until gradually you have stirred in all the liquid. The whole process takes about 20–25 minutes, by which time the rice will be thick and creamy and the other ingredients piping hot. Stir in the butter cut in small pieces and when it is melted, season the risotto with salt and pepper. Serve the cheese sprinkled on top.

Left-over risotto can be fried by heating a tablespoon of oil in a frying pan, adding the cold risotto and pressing it well down to form a flat cake. Cook over a low heat until the base is golden, about 10–15 minutes. Turn it over; it doesn't matter if it breaks up, simply press it well down again and fry for a further 10 minutes or so until the underside is golden brown.

Fish dishes

Baked fish

Almost any kind of fish can be baked and this is a good way of dealing with it when coping for several people. Simply lay your chosen fish (1 fish per person in the case of mackerel or herrings and 150–225 g (6–8 oz) per head of fish fillets or steaks) in a shallow oven dish, dot with butter or margarine and sprinkle with lemon juice and about 150 ml ($^1/_4$ pint) water, add perhaps a sprinkling of herbs and a few chopped cloves of garlic. Season with salt and pepper and put into a pre-heated oven for 15–25 minutes. Times vary according to size and thickness of the fish. It is done when the flesh turns opaque.

Chilli baked fish – serves 4

This is a more elaborate recipe for baking fish which is rich and spicy and is suitable for all sorts of fish including steaks, fillets and whole fish.

4 fish steaks, fillets or whole fish such as herrings,
mackerel or trout
lemon juice
1 onion, finely chopped
2 cloves garlic, chopped
1 can Italian chopped tomatoes
1 teaspoon dried oregano or mixed herbs
2 whole red chillies
salt and pepper
4 tablespoons breadcrumbs or wheatgerm
1 tablespoon oil

Lay the fish in a shallow oven-proof dish and sprinkle with a little lemon juice and the chopped onion and garlic. Pour over the can of tomatoes and add the herbs and chillies. Season with a little salt and pepper. Spread the breadcrumbs or wheatgerm evenly over the top and sprinkle with the oil. Heat the oven to Gas 6/400°F/200°C and bake for 40 minutes until hot and bubbling.

Squid with fiery mayonnaise – serves 4

Squid are cheap and delicious. This recipe is suitable for the small, ready-prepared variety that is sold by some fishmongers and super-markets.

700 g (1½ lbs) ready-prepared squid
salt and pepper
1 onion, chopped
2 cloves garlic, chopped
1 teaspoon dried mixed herbs
mayonnaise mixed with 1–2 cloves garlic, chopped

Cut the squid into rings and put them into a saucepan, season with salt and pepper and add the onion, garlic and herbs. Just cover with cold water. Bring to the boil, put on the lid and simmer for 1 hour. Eat with the garlic-flavoured mayonnaise.

Mussels in cider or apple juice – 2 servings

A soup bowl of mussels, eaten with copious amounts of French bread, provides a satisfying meal for 2. If you're feeding more, treat them as a starter and finish off the meal with something quick and simple such as an omelette. Mussels can contain a fair amount of sand. To rid them of this, put them in a bowl with 1 tablespoon of flour and leave for a few hours: they will open to eat the flour and shed their sand.

1 kg (2¼ lbs) mussels in their shells
2 cloves garlic or 1 small onion, chopped
pepper
150 ml (¼ pint) dry cider or apple juice
2–3 tablespoons chopped parsley, optional

Wash the mussels in two or three changes of water using a bowl, then scrub them under running cold water, pulling away the straggly beards. If any are open, tap sharply with a wooden spoon, if they won't close, discard as they will be dead, also discard any with broken shells. Put the garlic or onion, a seasoning of pepper, the cider and parsley into a large saucepan. Add the mussels. Cover and bring to the boil. Boil briskly for about 5 minutes until all the mussels have opened and they are piping hot.

Baked small fry

This recipe is suitable for small fish like sardines or sprats. Don't despise the latter – they are available during the winter months and are very cheap. Eat these fish with plenty of brown bread and butter. Sprats can be cooked ungutted but not sardines. You can buy them ready-prepared at some fish counters, otherwise carefully slit them open down the belly and remove all traces of the black gut.

150 g (6 oz) sardines or sprats per person
oil
lemon juice
$1/4$ teaspoon dried thyme or mixed herbs.
pepper

Heat oven to Gas 4/350°F/180°C. Lay the fish in an oven-proof dish and sprinkle with a little oil and lemon juice, the thyme and a little pepper. Bake for about 15 minutes. Sprinkle with a little more lemon juice before eating.

That Sunday roast

Occasionally, just occasionally, you might need to know how to roast a joint of meat. It's an expensive option but if there's a group to feed, you might feel that sometimes you'd like to enjoy the traditional Sunday lunch. So it's as well to know how to go about it.

If the meat has been frozen, make sure it is really thawed before you cook it and that it doesn't come straight from the fridge, but stands in the kitchen for at least 30 minutes before you put it into the oven. The table on page 128 gives roasting times but first the basic method:

joint beef, lamb or pork
2–3 tablespoons oil

Heat oven to specified temperature. Put the oil in the roasting tin and put it into the oven for 5 minutes. Put the meat in the tin and baste it by spooning some of the hot oil over it. Put the roasting tin in the oven on the centre shelf and baste the meat every 20–30 minutes (although pork, because it is fatty, doesn't need basting). At the end of the cooking time, turn the oven off and leave the meat for 15 minutes, which helps it to compact and makes it easier to carve.

Allow 100–175 g (4–6 oz) per head for a boneless joint and double that for a joint with a bone.

Gravy

To make gravy, once the joint is cooked remove it from the tin and pour away most of the cooking juices. Put the tin on top of the stove and pour in about 300 ml ($\frac{1}{2}$ pint, 1 mug) stock or water. Boil rapidly so that it reduces to about half, stirring all the time.

Mint sauce

Mix 2 tablespoons fresh chopped mint or 1 tablespoon dried with 1 teaspoon sugar. Pour over a little boiling water. When the sugar has dissolved add 6 tablespoons vinegar. Stir and set aside for 30 minutes before using.

Apple sauce

Peel and slice 3–4 apples and put them in a small pan with 1 tablespoon water and 1 tablespoon butter. Cook very gently for 30 minutes until they are soft. Mash with a fork.

Beef Choose topside or silverside – the more expensive sirloin and top rib are for when you win the lottery.	Heat oven to Gas 5/375°F/190°C and roast for 20 minutes per 450 g (1 lb) + 20 minutes.
Lamb Choose shoulder or leg. Don't despise New Zealand lamb which is usually cheaper. Make slits with a pointed knife and insert slivers of garlic or herbs like rosemary or thyme.	Heat oven to Gas 5/375°F/190°C and roast for 25 minutes per 450 g (1 lb) + 20 minutes.
Pork Choose boned and rolled shoulder or knuckle end. For crisp crackling, the fat must be deeply scored before cooking. Pour over 2–3 tablespoons of oil and rub in 1 tablespoon of salt. Pork must be well cooked. To test, insert a skewer or pointed knife into the thickest part, if the juice runs pink, cook a little longer.	Heat oven to Gas 7/425°F/220°C for the first 15 minutes, then lower heat to Gas 5/375°F/190°C. Cook for 30 minutes per 450 g (1 lb) + 20 minutes.

Yorkshire pudding

100 g (4 oz) plain flour
pinch salt
1 egg
300 ml (½ pint) mixture of milk and water

Put the flour and salt into a bowl. Make a hollow in the centre and break in the egg. Add 5 tablespoons of the liquid and begin to mix in the flour. Gradually add the remaining liquid, mixing until all the flour is incorporated and you have a thin, smooth batter. Beat well, using a whisk or wooden spoon, until it is frothy. Set aside for 1 hour before using to allow the flour to absorb the liquid. Beat well again before cooking.

To cook: 45 minutes before the meat is roasted, put 1 tablespoon of oil into a shallow oven-proof dish and set it in the oven on the top shelf for 5 minutes. Take it from the oven and pour the batter into it. Return to the oven for the remainder of the cooking time.

To roast vegetables

Potatoes and root vegetables like parsnips can be roasted round the joint. First skin, cut into even pieces and boil them for 5 minutes. Drain well and either put them round the joint or in a separate pan with a little hot oil. They will take about 1 hour.

Extras

Salads

Salads make the perfect base for a meal in a hurry and can be eaten at any time of the year using the whole gamut of salad greens and vegetables in season which, because they are eaten raw, retain all their nutrients. All you need to do to make a complete meal is to eat them with a good chunk of bread and something simple like a hard-boiled egg, or sliced cold meats such as ham, salami or other Continental sausage, or fish such as smoked mackerel, canned tuna or sardines, or two or three tablespoons of any canned or cooked pulses, or cheese, such as a dollop of curd or cottage or a hard cheese such as Cheddar, sliced or grated, or, for something special, goat's cheese.

Salad ingredients should be as fresh as possible and prepared just before they are eaten and, in order to retain their maximum goodness, they should be washed under running cold water and not left to soak. Salad greens like lettuce and spinach can simply be torn into manageable pieces, whereas other vegetables may need chopping or shredding. If you're not going to eat all of the vegetable at once, save the root end as it will remain fresher longer.

Salad dressings

All salads need some kind of dressing. Some are very easy and quite cheap to make whereas others like mayonnaise are more troublesome.

Vinaigrette

Make it with a wine or cider vinegar, not malt, which is too strong, or use lemon juice instead. Use a good quality oil like corn, sunflower, soya or peanut oil (olive oil is the best but it is very expensive).

1 tablespoon vinegar or lemon juice
6 tablespoons oil
salt and pepper

Put all the ingredients into a clean and dry screw-topped jar, put on the lid and shake well to mix. Or put the vinegar into a cup and gradually beat in the oil a tablespoon at a time and season with the salt and pepper.

Vary this dressing by adding one or two of the following: 1 teaspoon mustard, $1/2$ teaspoon tomato purée, 1 tablespoon pesto, few drops soy sauce, 1 tablespoon peanut butter, 2 tablespoons yogurt, $1/2$ teaspoon dried herbs or a tablespoon of fresh chopped herbs like parsley or sweet basil.

Yogurt dressing

Yogurt is a good base for salad dressings.

2–3 tablespoons plain yogurt
1 teaspoon lemon juice
1 clove garlic, finely chopped
$1/2$ teaspoon dried herbs or 1 tablespoon fresh, chopped, optional
salt and pepper

Mix the yogurt with all the other ingredients.

Yogurt

If you like yogurt, you'll know that it is not only delicious with salads but is good too with cereals and fruit or just on its own. So if you eat a lot you may like to try your hand at making your own, it's by far the cheapest option. My version uses *long-life* or *UHT milk*; if you use ordinary milk, it must be brought to boiling point and then cooled down. Make your yogurt either in a wide-mouthed insulated container with a lid, or in a bowl. (If you use a conventional vacuum flask make sure you don't bash it so hard when stirring that you shatter the glass!)

sufficient long-life milk to fill your flask, or 600 ml (1 pint)
    if using a bowl
1–2 tablespoons skimmed milk powder, optional
1 tablespoon ready-made natural (not pasteurized) yogurt

Heat the milk in a saucepan until it reaches blood temperature: the test is to be able to dip your finger in it and count to 10. Put the milk powder if using (it will produce a thicker yogurt) and the tablespoon of yogurt into a clean flask or bowl. Stir the warm milk into the mixture. Put on the lid of the flask and set aside. (Or cover the bowl with a clean cloth and put in a warm place.) Check after 4 hours. It should be set but it can take up to 8 hours. When it has set, pour the contents from the flask into a bowl. Put the bowl into the fridge to cool and stop the fermenting process.

To make the next batch, use a tablespoon of this yogurt as a starter. This can go on indefinitely, but if you find the results are becoming less good, buy a small, fresh pot and start again.

Cottage or curd cheese dressing

As above recipe for yogurt dressing but use cottage or curd cheese instead of yogurt.

Soy and lemon dressing

Simply mix equal quantities of soy sauce and lemon juice together.

Soy and peanut butter dressing

2 tablespoons soy sauce
2 tablespoons peanut butter
1 tablespoon oil
1 clove garlic, chopped
1 teaspoon lemon juice

Mix the soy sauce with the peanut butter, beat in the oil and add the garlic and lemon juice.

Mayonnaise

Don't despise bottled mayonnaise, especially some of the excellent supermarkets' *own brands*. Of course home-made is superior but, by the time you've bought all the ingredients, it doesn't work out much cheaper and although, once mastered, it is not difficult to make, it is one of those things that can cause frayed tempers until the knack is learnt. There's a detailed recipe in *Vegetarian Student*, but for the purposes of this book I'm suggesting you buy a jar of ready-made and eat it as it is or give it fire in one of the following ways.

Mix two or three tablespoons with a tablespoon of tomato purée or pesto, or add a dash of soy sauce, or a finely chopped clove of garlic and perhaps a teaspoon of chilli powder.

Mayonnaise and yogurt dressing

1 tablespoon mayonnaise
1 tablespoon yogurt

Mix the two together and add one of the following:
• *cheese, blue-veined* – 15 g (½ oz) mashed.
• *curry powder* – ½ teaspoon and a squeeze of lemon juice.
• *herbs* – 1 teaspoon dried or ½ tablespoon fresh, chopped.
• *mustard* – 1 teaspoon made.
• *tomato purée* or *tomato ketchup* – 1 teaspoon.

Ideas for salads

• *Apples* – chopped, crisp eating apples are delicious in most salads.
• *Avocados* – although not cheap, avocados are nutritious and filling. They are eaten when they are soft and you may sometimes find a greengrocer selling them off cheaply once they have reached this state. The easiest way to eat an avocado is to cut it in half, remove the stone, and fill the cavity with a salad dressing. Or if you prefer, halve it, remove the stone and cut it into quarters, when it's easy to peel away the skin. Then chop or slice it and eat with a dressing or combined with other salad vegetables. (Once cut, avocado flesh turns black, which can be inhibited by sprinkling it with lemon juice.)
• *Beansprouts* – eat them as they are or mixed with one or two of the following: chopped apple, onion, sweet pepper or mushrooms.
• *Beetroot* – buy the ready-cooked kind and slice or chop it. It goes well with yogurt dressing or vinaigrette, hard-boiled egg,

sardines, chopped apple, tomato and garlic.

- *Cabbage* – cut off just what you need from a white or red cabbage and shred it finely. Mix with vinaigrette, mayonnaise or yogurt dressing. It goes well with chopped apple, carrot, celery, sweet peppers, dried fruit, chopped nuts, sliced onion, a tablespoon or two of pulses.
- *Carrot* – grate or slice and mix with a dressing or simply some lemon juice. Nice with finely chopped onion, garlic or sliced orange and chicory.
- *Cauliflower* – cut off a few florets and mix with vinaigrette or mayonnaise flavoured with mustard.
- *Celeriac* – peel and grate. Mix with vinaigrette or yogurt dressing.
- *Celery* – peel away outer fibres, cut into 2.5 cm (1 in) lengths. It goes well with chopped apple, nuts, grated carrot, sliced or grated cheese, cooked potato and sweet pepper.
- *Chicory* – wipe and slice. Good with grated carrot, sliced orange and a lemon flavoured vinaigrette.
- *Chinese leaves* – slice off what you need from the top end. Mix with vinaigrette.
- *Courgette* – slice, chop or grate. Goes well with vinaigrette, chopped onion or garlic and grated cheese.
- *Cucumber* – slice or dice. Goes well with cottage cheese, yogurt, mint, chives.
- *Dried fruit, nuts and seeds* – these all add interest and nutrition to salads. Add a tablespoon or two of dried fruit and nuts or a sprinkling of sunflower, pumpkin, sesame or melon seeds.
- *Endive* – looks like frizzy lettuce and has a slightly bitter flavour. Use like lettuce.
- *Fennel* – wipe over and slice. Nice with sliced cheese, grated carrot and a vinaigrette.
- *French beans* – wash and chop and mix with vinaigrette.
- *Garlic, spring onions and chives* – all add a pungent flavour to salads. Garlic should be chopped finely. Spring onions should be washed, the green stems cut away and discarded. They can be left

whole or sliced. Chives can be grown in a pot on a window-sill. Using scissors, cut off a few of the green stems and snip them into small pieces over your chosen salad.

- *Herbs* – chopped fresh herbs like parsley, chervil, dill, mint and basil make salads more interesting. They're worth buying in pots and keeping on a window-sill.
- *Lettuce* – there's a vast selection of lettuces on sale, some very expensive. A plain and simple round lettuce is not to be despised, especially if you eat it with a good dressing. Wash it well and get rid of as much of the excess water as possible by shaking it in a clean tea-towel or colander. Keep what you don't need in a plastic bag or wrapped in newspaper at the bottom of the fridge or in a cool, dark place.
- *Mangetout* – wash and slice and mix with vinaigrette.
- *Mushrooms* – slice or leave small ones whole. Mix with vinaigrette or yogurt dressing with a little chopped garlic. They go well with chickpeas or other pulses and fish such as tuna or mussels.
- *Radishes* – delicious dipped in salt and butter.
- *Spinach* – wash well and tear the leaves into shreds. Nice with a sliced hard-boiled egg and a sprinkling of chopped garlic or spring onions and a vinaigrette dressing.
- *Tomatoes* – slice and sprinkle with vinaigrette dressing perhaps mixed with a little pesto. Nice with fresh herbs, especially basil and a generous sprinkling of chopped garlic, spring onions or chives. Delicious eaten with sliced goat's, cottage or curd cheese.

Salads with cooked vegetables

If you cook more vegetables than you need for one meal, you can use the rest to make some interesting salads. If you add a dressing to them while they are still warm, they will absorb much more of its flavour.

Salads with pulses

Most cooked pulses are delicious in salads, especially if flavoured with a little chopped garlic or onion.

Salads with cooked rice and pasta

When you cook too much of either, mix them while still warm with a vinaigrette and use them as a base for a cold meal the next day mixed with one or two of the following: a sliced tomato, canned tuna fish, sardines, mussels or pilchards, shredded cooked meat like ham or salami, sliced mushrooms, a tablespoon or two of canned or cooked pulses or some beansprouts. Add flavour with chopped garlic and herbs like mint, parsley or basil.

Beansprouts to grow

Almost any kind of dried bean can be used for sprouting with the exception of split lentils or split peas. The most usual kind to use is mung beans.

2 tablespoons mung or other beans

Wash the beans and put them into a wide-mouthed, clean jar. Cover with cold water and leave to soak for 8 hours or overnight. Rinse them again until the water runs clear and return them to the jar. Cover the top with a clean piece of cloth (this can be muslin, a piece of J-cloth or a handerchief) and secure with a rubber band. Lay the jar on its side and leave it somewhere where the water can drain out. The beans must be moist but not swimming or they will go mouldy. Once in the morning and once in the evening, fill the jar with fresh water and put it once again on its side to drain. 3–4 days later, the beans will have sprouted and the pale, cream tendrils will fill the jar. Rinse them and put them into a bowl, covered, and store in the fridge.

Eat within 4–5 days and start a second batch.

Vegetables

It's a fact of life that many people think vegetables are boring, probably because of being told they are good for you and being made to eat them up. However, properly treated, they are delicious, very easy to prepare and, with judicious seasoning, they add an essential extra to a meal.

Fresh, seasonal vegetables are the best option but if you have access to a freezer frozen vegetables are a great standby and, because they are frozen as soon as they are picked, they retain most of their nutrients. Vegetables that are canned do suffer from a change in texture and flavour but when you're in a hurry, they are not to be despised. Jazz them up with a bit of extra flavouring, see page 142.

Preparing fresh vegetables

In order to preserve their vitamins and nutrients, vegetables should be prepared just before you use them. They should be washed, preferably under running cold water, and not be left to soak for hours. Appetites vary but as a rough guide allow 100–150 g (4–6 oz) per head except for peas, broad beans and spinach, when you should allow at least double this amount. When peeling vegetables, it is helpful to use a swivel-bladed peeler which is able to pare away the skin very finely. However, thick-skinned vegetables like swedes are easier to peel with a knife.

The following table shows how to prepare different vegetables and gives their approximate cooking times. After the table are instructions on how to boil and steam vegetables together with some ideas for seasoning them.

Vegetable	Preparation	Boiling time in minutes	Steaming time in minutes
Broad beans	Shell.	15–20	20–25
Broccoli	Divide into florets and discard any hard stalks.	10–15	15–20
Brussels sprouts	Trim stalk end, discard yellowing leaves.	5–10	10–15
Cabbage white and green	Quarter, or cut in strips, cut away woody stalk.	5	10
Carrots	Cut off head and tail, peel, slice or quarter.	10–15	15–20
Cauliflower	As broccoli.		
Chicory	Cut root end, cook whole.	10–15	15–20
Corn on the cob	Peel off green leaves and white fibres. Add no salt to cooking water. Eat with lots of melted butter.	20–25	25–30
Courgettes	Cut off ends, slice, or cook small ones whole.	5–10	10–15
Fennel	Cut off root, wipe over and slice or quarter.	10–15	15–20
French beans	Top, tail and remove stringy bits.	10–15	15–20

Vegetable	Preparation	Boiling time in minutes	Steaming time in minutes
Greens	Discard coarse outer leaves, cut in strips.	5	10
Jerusalem artichokes	Cook in skins.	10–15	15–20
Kale	As greens.		
Leeks	Discard root end and all but 5 cm (2 in) of green top. Can be gritty, so slit in half before washing. Slice.	10–15	15–20
Mangetout	Top and tail.	10–15	15–20
Okra	As mangetout.	10–15	15–20
Parsnips	Peel and cut off ends. Quarter or slice.	10–15	15–20
Peas	As broad beans.		
Potatoes	Peel and cut into even-sized pieces about the size of an egg.	20–25	25–30
Runner beans	As French beans, but cut into small lengths.	10–15	15–20
Spinach	Wash thoroughly and cook with no added water.	5	10
Sugarsnap peas	As mangetout.	10–15	15–20
Swedes	As parsnips.	10–15	15–20
Turnips	As parsnips.	10–15	15–20

Boiling vegetables

To boil vegetables, put them into a saucepan, just cover with boiling water, add a pinch of salt, bring to the boil. Lower the heat, put on a lid and leave to simmer for the specified time, see table on pages 140–1. Drain well (remember the cooking water can be used for stock) and add seasonings, see below. (If you keep the cooking water, you can use it as a stock.)

Steaming vegetables

To steam vegetables you will need a steamer, the collapsible basket kind is the cheapest and most convenient. Put the steamer in a saucepan with just sufficient water to come up to its base. Add the prepared vegetable, cover the pan, bring the water to the boil, lower the heat and steam until the vegetables are just tender, as in the table above. You can steam one or more vegetables at the same time, either choosing ones which take the same time to cook, or beginning with the one that takes the longest and adding others at the appropriate moment. Lift the steamer out of the saucepan, using a cloth so as not to burn yourself, and let it stand for a minute or two for the vegetables to drain. Add seasonings, see below. (Remember the cooking water can be used in place of stock.)

Seasoning boiled or steamed vegetables

Most boiled or steamed vegetables, whether fresh, canned or frozen, become something special with the addition of a knob of butter or margarine or a tablespoon of yogurt stirred in. Season them with salt and pepper and perhaps a pinch of nutmeg and either a squeeze of lemon juice or a few drops soy sauce. Fresh chopped herbs add to their appeal: try either parsley, mint, chives, basil, oregano or thyme. If no fresh herbs are available add a pinch or two of dried.

Baked vegetables

Certain vegetables, like potatoes, lend themselves to baking. They include potatoes, onions, sweet potatoes, tomatoes, mushrooms and

Vegetable	Preparation	Baking time
Mushrooms	Lay large flat mushrooms in an oven-proof dish. Put a knob of butter on each, add salt, pepper and a sprinkling of herbs like thyme or parsley.	10–15 minutes
Onions	Bake whole in skins, cutting off a little from each end.	1 – 1½ hours
Potatoes	Prick with a fork or cut a cross on one side and, to speed up cooking time, push a skewer right through the centre.	1 hour
Sweet potatoes	As potatoes.	1¼ – 1½ hours
Tomatoes, large	Cut in half, put in an oven-proof dish, sprinkle with a little salt and pepper and dried herbs, some finely chopped garlic and a little oil.	10 minutes
Yams	Peel, rub with oil and prick with a fork, insert a skewer through the centre to speed up cooking time.	1¼ hours

yams. The following table shows preparation and approximate cooking times which may vary a little according to the size of the vegetable. The oven should be heated to Gas 6–7/400–425°F/200–220°C.

Braised vegetables

Some vegetables can be braised in the oven, which is useful if you are already using it for something else. Suitable vegetables are carrots, leeks, fennel, celery, potatoes and most root vegetables. They should be sliced and then boiled for a few minutes before being drained and transferred to a shallow oven-proof dish. Just cover them with boiling water and season with salt and pepper and perhaps a dash of soy sauce and a sprinkling of dried mixed herbs or a little cumin, fennel or coriander.

Put them into an oven heated to Gas 6/400°F/200°C and let them cook until soft, about 1 hour.

Cauliflower cheese – serves 4

Serve cauliflower cheese when you're cooking for more than one, either as a vegetable or a cheap meal in itself, in which case one medium cauliflower will do for 2. If you haven't the time or inclination to make the cheese sauce, you could always buy a *sauce mix*, or top the cauliflower with a liberal dose of grated cheese and brown it under the grill.

1 cauliflower, divided into florets, hard stalk discarded
salt
cheese sauce, see below
2 tablespoons grated cheese

Put about 1 cm (½ in) water into a saucepan, bring to the boil, add a pinch of salt and the florets. Cover and simmer until tender, 5–10 minutes. Drain well. Meanwhile make the cheese sauce. Put the drained cauliflower into an oven-proof dish, pour over the sauce and sprinkle the grated cheese all over. Brown under a hot grill or in an oven heated to Gas 7/425°F/220°C for 5–10 minutes.

Cheese sauce

The following method is a somewhat unorthodox way of making a cheese sauce but it is easier than the classic method and results in a smooth, creamy sauce free from lumps.

300 ml (½ pint, 1 mug) milk
25g (1 oz) butter, oil or margarine

25 g (1 oz) flour
salt and pepper
3–4 tablespoons grated or curd cheese
pinch nutmeg, optional

Put the milk with the butter, oil or margarine into a small saucepan and sprinkle in the flour. Stand the pan over a medium heat and stir constantly as the contents heat, using either a whisk or a wooden spoon, making sure that the flour is amalgamated with the liquid and no lumps form. As the sauce begins to thicken and nears boiling point, lower the heat but continue to stir. After it begins to bubble, it must be stirred for a further 2 minutes. Remove from the heat, season with salt and pepper and stir in the cheese, and nutmeg if using. As soon as it has melted, the sauce is ready to serve.

Potato and leek gratin

The combination of these two vegetables makes a wonderfully satisfying dish to be eaten perhaps with some sliced cold ham or grilled sausages.

2 tablespoons oil
2 leeks, well washed and sliced
700 g (1 ½ lbs) potatoes, peeled and sliced
salt and pepper
1 teaspoon dried thyme or mixed herbs
approximately 300 ml (½ pint, 1 mug) stock or water
25 g (1 oz) butter or margarine

Heat the oil in a flame-proof gratin dish or casserole and fry the sliced leeks very gently for about 10 minutes. Heat the oven to Gas 6/400°F/200°C. Peel and slice the potatoes and mix with the leeks. Season with a little salt and pepper and the dried thyme or mixed herbs. Pour over sufficient stock or water barely to cover. Bring to the boil. Put little dots of butter or margarine on top and put into the oven for 50–60 minutes until the top layer of potatoes is golden brown.

Red cabbage

This is a cheap and cheerful vegetable in the depths of winter, but it needs long, slow cooking, so it's really only worth doing if there are several of you eating, although in fact it does reheat well. Incidentally, red cabbage is delicious shredded and eaten raw in salads.

1 small red cabbage, quartered
salt and pepper
2 tablespoons vinegar
25 g (1 oz) margarine or butter
2 eating apples
1 tablespoon sugar

Cut away the hard stalk and shred the cabbage finely. Put it into a deep saucepan with a pinch of salt, some pepper, the vinegar and margarine or butter. Cover the pan, put over a low heat and cook for 1 hour. After this time, peel, quarter and core the apples and mix them into the cabbage with the sugar. Cover again and continue to cook slowly for a further hour.

Ratatouille

This makes a great summer vegetable dish and is just as delicious cold as it is hot. Exact quantities are not obligatory but it does need a good assortment of different Mediterranean vegetables.

4 tablespoons oil
1–2 onions
1–2 aubergines, chopped
1–2 courgettes, sliced
1–2 sweet peppers, deseeded and sliced
1 can Italian chopped tomatoes
2 cloves garlic, chopped
salt and pepper
1 teaspoon dried thyme or mixed herbs

Use a large saucepan, add the oil and when it is hot put in the vegetables in the order given, mixing them together with a wooden spoon. Add the garlic, salt, pepper and thyme or mixed herbs. Bring slowly to the boil, cover and simmer for 1 hour. Remove the lid and simmer for a further 30 minutes or so in order to evaporate most of the liquid.

Everyday drinks

Tea

It's up to you whether you buy loose tea or teabags. Loose is cheaper but it tends to clog up the sink. Instant tea is more expensive than either. Teabags don't need a pot but neither does loose if you buy a tea infuser, which is sold in specialist tea shops and nearly always on a stall at every boot sale. The secret of good tea is freshly boiled water.

Iced tea – refreshing in summer. Make strong tea, let it cool and add a lump or two of ice and perhaps a sprig of mint and a slice of lemon.

Herb teas – a huge selection on sale, especially in health shops. You either love or hate them, so try them out at someone else's place before you lash out and buy some!

Coffee

Most students find it hard to live without coffee, which is unfortunate as it has become uncomfortably expensive. And, what is worse with coffee, you really do get what you pay for. This is especially true of *instant*, which is likely to be your first choice. But if you do decide to buy fresh ground coffee, it is as well to know how to make it. Unlike tea, coffee should be made with water just off the boil.

Coffee made in a jug

This method requires no special equipment and many consider it the best.

water
1 tablespoon medium ground coffee per mug

Boil the water and warm the jug by pouring in a little and letting it stand for a moment or two before pouring it away. Put the coffee into the jug and pour over 300 ml (½ pint) of water per mug. The water should not be boiling. Stir well and leave for 3–4 minutes for the grounds to settle. If there are still grounds floating on the surface, sprinkle a few drops of cold water on top and drag the base of a spoon over it. You may find you need to use a strainer when you pour the coffee.

If you like this method, look out for a glass cafetière which comes with its own built-in filter plunger. The coffee is placed in the warmed jug, water is poured over and the filter attached to the plunger is rested on top. After 4 minutes, the plunger is pushed down so that the filter is pressed to the bottom of the jug, taking all the grounds to the base.

Filter coffee

An alternative to the above is to buy a plastic filter cone and a pack of filter papers. When the water comes to the boil, warm the jug and stand the filter cone lined with a paper on top of it and pour in a few drops of water. When this has been absorbed, add required amount of coffee, see recipe above. Dampen the coffee with a little water before filling the filter right to the top with more water, topping it up as the filter absorbs it, until you have added sufficient water for the number of mugs.

Iced coffee

Wonderful in the summer. Simply make extra-strong coffee and sweeten to taste while it is still hot. Let it cool completely and put in the fridge. To drink, top it with a dollop of vanilla ice cream.

Cocoa and hot chocolate

Cocoa is cheaper than drinking chocolate, which contains a lot of sweetener. Follow instructions on packets. A little powdered cinnamon sprinkled over the top adds a subtle flavour.

Hot chocolate with coffee

Either put 1 teaspoon instant coffee and 2 teaspoons drinking chocolate into a mug and pour over hot milk *or* make instant coffee with milk instead of water and grate plain chocolate over the top.

Lemon with honey

This is comforting for a streaming cold. You can use an orange instead of the lemon and, of course, if you can add a dash of whisky, this will add to the benefits!

1 lemon
boiling water
1 teaspoon honey

Cut the lemon in half and squeeze the juice into a cup, scooping out the pips. Top up with boiling water and stir in the honey.

Orangeade or lemonade

This is great in hot weather and will keep well in the fridge for several days. It must be made a day ahead so that the liquid can absorb the flavour of the fruit.

600 ml (1 pint, 2 mugs) boiling water
2 oranges or 2 lemons
2–3 tablespoons sugar

Put the water into a bowl. Grate the rind from the lemons or the oranges on top, taking care not to include any of the pith, stir in the sugar and cover with a cloth or lid. Leave overnight. Next day, cut the fruit in half and squeeze the juice into the bowl. Taste and if necessary add a little more sugar. Strain into a jug. Drink as it is or dilute to taste with more water.

Lemon barley water

4 tablespoons barley flakes
1 tablespoon sugar
1 lemon
300 ml (½ pint, 1 mug) boiling water

Put the barley flakes and sugar into a bowl. Cut the lemon in half, squeeze in the juice and then add the halved fruit. Pour over the boiling water. Leave overnight. The next day strain into a jug and keep cool. Dilute as required with water.

Citron and orange pressé

If you can't be bothered with the above, do as the French do and simply squeeze the juice of an orange or lemon into a glass, add lots of ice and top up with water and add sugar to taste.

Yogurt drinks

If the idea of yogurt drinks seems bizarre, think of the Indian *lassi* and how delicious this is with curry. *Lassi* is made by putting two tablespoons of yogurt into a glass and topping up with cold water and ice. It is flavoured with a pinch of cumin and salt. In Iran they have a similar drink called *abelidoh,* which is made in the same way but with soda water instead of plain water. A variation on the theme is to use fruit juice instead of water.

Party drinks

Parties mean alcohol and alcohol is expensive. It can be made less so by using it in punches and the like. You can devise your own mixtures but be wary of mixing different kinds of alcohol unless you don't mind everyone being sick all over your floor.

As a guide to how much to make: 1 litre (1¾ pints) will give about 8 glasses.

White wine and orange cup

2 litres dry white wine
1 can frozen concentrated orange juice
2 oranges, sliced
1 litre (1¾ pints) fizzy lemonade
ice cubes

Put wine, frozen juice and sliced oranges in a bowl. Leave 30 minutes. Add the lemonade and ice cubes.

Sangria – red wine and lemonade

1 orange, sliced
1 lemon, sliced
1 bottle red wine
1 litre (1¾ pints) fizzy lemonade
1 tablespoon sugar

Put all the ingredients into a bowl and mix.

Cider cup

1 litre (1¾ pints) strong dry cider
1 litre (1¾ pints) orange squash
½ bottle lemon squash
1 orange and 1 lemon, sliced
sprigs of mint

Put all the ingredients into a bowl and mix.

Warming drinks for winter

In the winter a mulled wine, spiced ale or hot punch are welcoming. The secret is to remove them from the heat as soon as the top begins to be flecked with white. Boiling will simply burn off the alcohol.

Mulled wine

1 litre (1¾ pints) red wine
1 orange stuck with 3 cloves
2 tablespoons sugar
½ teaspoon powdered cinnamon
½ teaspoon powdered nutmeg

Put all the ingredients into a pan and heat gently. As soon as the top is flecked with white remove from the heat. Spoon into warm glasses.

Spiced ale

1 litre (1¾ pints) brown ale
¼ bottle sweet white wine
300 ml (½ pint) apple juice
½ teaspoon ground ginger
½ teaspoon cinnamon

Put all the ingredients into a pan and heat gently. As soon as the top is flecked with white remove from the heat. Spoon into warm glasses.

Punch

1 bottle medium-dry Montilla
1 bottle dry white wine
1 litre (1¾ pints) orange juice
1 litre (1¾ pints) pineapple juice
1 tablespoon sugar

$^1/_2$ teaspoon powdered cinnamon
strip lemon or orange peel
2 oranges, sliced

Put all the ingredients except the sliced oranges into a pan and heat gently. As soon as the top is flecked with white remove from the heat. Add the sliced orange. Spoon into warm glasses.

How to minimize the effects of too much drink

Drink lots of water either between glasses of alcohol or before you go to bed because alcohol causes dehydration. If you know you are going to drink and there isn't going to be any food, line your stomach by drinking a glass of milk before you start.

Easy puddings

This is for indulgence. It's for those days when you want to treat yourself or your friends with a gooey pudding or some easy cakes. Most of these puddings are nice with something like cream, smetana, yogurt or fromage frais.

Fried bananas

25–50 g (1–2 oz) butter depending on numbers
1 banana per person, peeled and cut in half lengthways
1 tablespoon either marmalade, honey or sugar, per person

Heat the butter in a frying pan and when it is foaming add the banana(s). Fry gently until they are soft and top with the marmalade, honey or sugar.

Or ring the changes by adding a spoonful of chopped nuts or dried fruit and a sprinkling of cinnamon or nutmeg.

Fried apple or pear slices

25–50 g (1–2 oz) butter depending on numbers
1 apple or pear per person, peeled, quartered and cored and cut in slices
1 tablespoon sugar per person
sprinkling either cinnamon, nutmeg or mixed spice

Heat the butter in a frying pan and when it is foaming add the slices of apple, sugar and a sprinkling of cinnamon, nutmeg or mixed spice. Fry gently until they are soft.

Battered fruit – 4 servings

100 g (4 oz, 12 level tablespoons) plain flour
1 egg
300 ml (½ pint) mixture of milk and water

225 g (8 oz) fruit, peeled and sliced, see below
1 tablespoon oil
4 tablespoons sugar

Heat the oven to Gas 6/400°F/200°C. Put the flour into a bowl, make a hollow in the centre and break in the egg. Using a wooden spoon gradually incorporate it into the flour. Add the liquid a little at a time and keep stirring until you have a thin batter with no lumps. Beat well. Put the oil into a shallow oven dish or tin and put it into the oven to heat for about 4 minutes. Remove it using a cloth, put the fruit over the base and pour in the batter. Cook in the centre of the oven for 35–40 minutes when the batter will be risen and golden. Eat hot, warm or cold.

Choose from such fruit as: apples, pears, bananas, plums, cherries or blackberries. The apples and pears must be quartered, cored, peeled and sliced; the bananas peeled and sliced; the plums halved and stoned; the cherries and blackberries can be cooked whole.

Apple crumble – 4 servings

In a hurry, make the topping with a packet of crumble mix.

450 g (1 lb) apples, quartered, cored, peeled and sliced
225 g (8 oz) flour
100 g (4 oz) butter or margarine, cut into small pieces
100 g (4 oz) sugar

Heat oven to Gas 5/375°F/190°C. Lay the prepared apples in a shallow oven-proof dish. Put the flour into a bowl, add the butter and, using your fingers, rub the two together until they look like breadcrumbs. Stir in the sugar. Sprinkle this mixture evenly over the fruit and put into the oven for 30 minutes until the top is golden brown.

This recipe can be used for other fruit including pears and summer berries like raspberries and redcurrants. One of the nicest crumbles is to use a half-and-half mixture of apples and blackberries.

Crusty pears – 4 servings

450 g (1 lb) pears, peeled, quartered and sliced
50 g (2 oz) butter
4 slices bread
lemon juice
2 tablespoons sugar

Heat the oven to Gas 6/400°F/200°C. Grease a shallow oven-proof
dish with a little butter and spread the remainder over the bread.
Lay these in the dish and put the pear quarters on top, sprinkling
them with a little lemon juice as you go. Sprinkle over the sugar.
Put into the oven for 15–20 minutes.

Bread and butter pudding – 4 servings

6 thin slices of buttered bread
2 tablespoons any sort of dried fruit
2 eggs
300 ml (½ pint, 1 mug) milk
2 tablespoons sugar

Lay two slices of bread in a shallow oven dish and sprinkle over 1
tablespoon of dried fruit. Lay two more slices on top and sprinkle
with remaining dried fruit. Lay remaining two slices of bread on
top. Beat the eggs and beat in the milk. Pour this mixture over the
pudding and set aside for half an hour so that the bread can absorb
the liquid.

Heat the oven to Gas 4/350°F/180°C. Put the pudding into the
oven and after 20 minutes, remove the dish from the oven using a
cloth, sprinkle over the sugar and return to the oven. Leave a further 10–15 minutes until it is risen and golden.

Baked apples

1 apple weighing about 225 g (8 oz) per person
2 tablespoons water

1–2 teaspoons dried fruit, honey or chopped nuts per person,
   optional

Heat the oven to Gas 4/350°F/180°C. Carefully cut out the core of
each apple using a sharp knife so that there is a hollow right down
the middle. Pare a thin rind of peel all round each apple. Fill the
cavity of each with dried fruit, honey or chopped nuts, if using. Put
them into a shallow oven-proof dish and pour round the water.
Bake for 30–40 minutes or until they are soft.

Biscuit flan with summer fruits – 4 servings

You can use this simple biscuit flan as a base for all sorts of fruit
toppings such as blackberries, strawberries, raspberries, redcurrants and blackberries.

100 g (4 oz) digestive or ginger nut biscuits
50 g (2 oz) butter or margarine
225 g (8 oz) of your chosen fruit
150 ml (¼ pint) thick cream
150 ml (¼ pint) fromage frais

Crush the biscuits by putting them into a plastic bag and crushing
with a rolling pin or bottle. Melt the butter or margarine and mix it
with the crumbs. Turn the mixture into a flan tin measuring 20 cm
(8 in) and spread it firmly over the whole base, pressing down with
the back of a spoon. Put it into the fridge for 30 minutes to set. Beat
the cream with the fromage frais until thick, mix with the fruit and
pile on to the biscuit base.

Banana toffee pie

Use the above biscuit base to make a Banoffee pie. Condensed milk
is simmered until it thickens and turns a deep toffee colour before
being piled on to the base with bananas and cream.

1 can condensed milk

biscuit base, as above
150 ml (¹⁄₄ pint) double cream
2 bananas, sliced

Stand the can of condensed milk in a saucepan half filled with water and bring to the boil. Simmer for 2 hours, checking that there is always a sufficient level of water and topping up as necessary with more boiling water. Allow to cool sufficiently to handle before opening the can. Whip the cream with a whisk or fork in a deep bowl until thick. Spread the thickened condensed milk over the base, top with slices of banana and a final layer of whipped cream.

Chocolate mousse – 4 servings (a recipe for those who don't mind eating raw eggs!)

This is everyone's favourite. The first time you make it, you may feel alarmed at the various processes but, once you master it, you will want to produce this mousse at every possible excuse. Do remember that when you separate the eggs you must make absolutely sure none of the yolk goes into the whites or they will not beat successfully.

150 g (6 oz) plain chocolate
1 tablespoon water
3 eggs

Melt the chocolate with the water by putting it into a bowl and either setting it into a very low oven Gas 2/300°F/150°C for about 10 minutes or by standing it over a saucepan half filled with simmering water.

Separate the eggs. To do this crack each one sharply across the middle with the blade of a knife. Carefully separate the two halves and let the white ooze into a large bowl, tipping the two half shells from side to side so that the yolk passes from one to the other without breaking. Put the yolks into a separate bowl. Add the melted chocolate to the egg yolks and beat with a fork until they are mixed and gleaming.

Using a whisk or fork beat the egg whites with a wide, circular motion, the idea being to beat as much air as possible into the whites so that they lift and thicken and turn opaque. It's wrist-aching but rewarding! As soon as the whites are stiff, drop them into the chocolate mixture and, using a cutting and folding motion, incorporate the two together. Don't stir or try to hurry: you want to keep as much of the beaten-in air as possible. When the whole mixture is uniformly dark, pour it into four glasses. Put in the fridge to set for at least 1 hour.

Summer pudding – 4 servings

This must be made a day ahead for the fruit and juices to penetrate the lining of bread.

450 g (1 lb) mixture of soft summer fruits such as raspberries, red- or blackcurrants, loganberries or blackberries
6 tablespoons sugar
stale white bread to line the basin

Put the fruit and sugar into a saucepan, bring to the boil and simmer for 3 minutes. Set aside.

Use a small, deep bowl which will hold about 600 ml (1 pint) and line the base and sides with 5mm ($1/4$ in) slices of bread, plugging any gaps with small pieces of bread. Pour in the fruit and juices and cover with more pieces of bread. Put a small plate on top and weigh this down with something heavy (a couple of tins perhaps). Put in the fridge until the next day.

To turn out, remove weight and plate and run a knife all round the sides of the bowl, invert a large plate on top and quickly, so as not to lose the juice, reverse the pudding on to the plate.

Quick biscuits and tea breads

Date crunchies

2 mugs porridge oats
75 g (3 oz) soft margarine
75 g (3 oz, 6 tablespoons) sugar
$^1/_4$ teaspoon nutmeg
$^1/_4$ teaspoon cinnamon
225 g (8 oz) chopped dates

Heat oven to Gas 4/350°F/180°C. Using a fork mix the oats with the soft margarine in a bowl. Stir in the sugar, nutmeg and cinnamon. Grease a flan tin with a little butter or oil, put half the mixture in it and using the back of a spoon press it all over the base. Sprinkle the chopped dates all over and cover with the other half of the mixture, pressing it flat with the spoon. Bake for 15 minutes. Remove from the oven and mark it into 12 wedges. Leave to cool, then cut through the wedges and transfer them to a plate or airtight container. (If they stick put back into the warm oven for a few minutes.)

Flapjacks

75 g (3 oz) margarine
75 g (3 oz, 6 tablespoons) sugar
2 tablespoons golden syrup
1$^1/_2$ mugs porridge oats

Heat oven to Gas 5/375°F/190°C. Melt the margarine with the sugar and golden syrup in a saucepan over a low heat. When they have melted, gradually mix in the porridge oats. Grease a flan tin, put the mixture in it and spread it evenly over the base using the back of a spoon. Bake for 15 minutes. Let it cool a little and mark into 12 wedges with a knife. Remove from tin before it is completely cold, otherwise it will stick. If it does, put it back in the still warm oven for a little before trying again. Put on to a plate or store in an airtight container.

Banana and walnut bread

Both this and the following *Peanut butter bread* are better still if kept a day before cutting. They can be stored, wrapped in foil, in the fridge. Eat them as they are or spread with margarine or butter and maybe a little honey, cheese or chocolate spread.

50 g (2 oz) margarine
100 g (4 oz) sugar
225 g (8 oz) plain flour (1 mug + 6 tablespoons)
3 teaspoons baking powder
50 g (2 oz) chopped walnuts
2 bananas
1 egg

Heat oven to Gas 4/350°F/180°C. Melt the margarine and sugar together in a small saucepan over a low heat. Put flour and baking powder into a bowl. Make a hollow in the centre and pour in the melted margarine and sugar. Mix with the blade of a knife and stir in the walnuts. Peel and mash the bananas and mix into the mixture. Break the egg into a cup, beat it with a fork, then stir it into the mixture. Grease a small loaf tin with butter or margarine, sprinkle in 1 tablespoon flour and shake the tin so that the flour coats the base and sides. Put mixture into it and smooth the top. Bake for 1 hour and test if it is cooked by piercing the centre with a skewer or pointed knife: if it comes out clean, the bread is done. If not, let it cook a little longer. Let the bread cool for 10 minutes in the tin before turning out and setting aside to get cold.

Peanut butter bread

225 g (8 oz; 1 mug + 6 tablespoons) plain flour
3 teaspoons baking powder

6 tablespoons peanut butter
6 tablespoons sugar
300 ml ($\frac{1}{2}$ pint, 1 mug) milk
2 tablespoons plain yogurt

Heat oven to Gas 4/350°F/180°C. Mix the flour and baking powder in a bowl. Make a hollow in the centre and add the peanut butter and mix using a fork. Stir in the sugar, milk and yogurt and beat hard for 2–3 minutes.

Grease a small loaf tin with butter or margarine, sprinkle in 1 tablespoon flour and shake the tin so that the flour coats the base and sides. Put mixture into the tin and smooth the top evenly. Bake for 1 hour and test if it is cooked by piercing the centre with a skewer or pointed knife: if it comes out clean, the bread is done. If not cook a little longer. Cool it for 10 minutes, then turn out of the tin.

Index